HIDDEN
EVIDENCE

40 TRUE CRIMES AND HOW FORENSIC SCIENCE HELPED SOLVE THEM

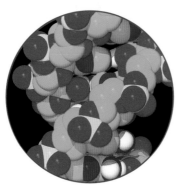

DAVID OWEN

FIREFLY BOOKS

A FIREFLY BOOK

Published by Firefly Books Ltd, 2000

Third Printing, 2000

Canadian Cataloguing-in-Publication Data
Owen, David, 1939-
    Hidden Evidence : 40 true crimes and how forensic science helped solve
them
Includes index.
ISBN 1-55209-483-9
1. Forensic sciences. 2. Criminal investigation. 3. Crime. I. Title.
HV8073.O93 2000   363.25   C00-930002-3

U.S. Cataloging-in-Publication Data
Owen, David
    Hidden evidence : 40 true crimes and how forensic
science helped solve them / David Owen. ——1st ed.
[240] p. : col. ill. ; cm..
Includes bibliographic resources and index.
Summary: the development of forensic science in
solving crimes, with real-life case examples.
ISBN 1-55209-483-9
1. Forensic sciences. 2. Criminal investigation.
3. Criminal psychology. I. Title.
363.25 –dc21   2000   CIP

Published in Canada in 2000 by
Firefly Books Ltd
3680 Victoria Park Avenue
Willowdale, Ontario
M2H 3K1

Published in the United States in 2000 by
Firefly Books (U.S.) Inc.
P.O. Box 1338, Ellicott Station
Buffalo, New York
14205

This book was designed and produced by
Quintet Publishing Limited
6 Blundell Street
London N7 7BH

Creative Director: Richard Dewing
Art Director: Simon Daley
Designer: James Lawrence
Senior Project Editor: Toria Leitch
Editor: Diane Pengelly
Picture Editor: Veneta Bullen

Typeset in Great Britain by
Central Southern Typesetters, Eastbourne

Manufactured in Hong Kong by Regent Publishing Services Ltd
Printed in Hong Kong by Midas Printing

Contents

Foreword

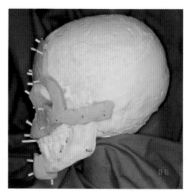

Hidden Evidence is a fascinating book. It focuses on the development and evolution of the techniques and technologies used in forensic criminal investigation, from the recognition of the uniqueness of fingerprints some 3,000 years ago in ancient China, to the present-day use of computerized DNA analysis. Each forensic subject is illustrated with synoptic examples using famous or infamous cases that will be familiar, to some degree, to most readers. Some of the cases cited occurred here in Los Angeles, where I have lived and worked since 1952. As I was reading, I reminisced of the days when I was involved in the investigations surrounding the deaths of Marilyn Monroe, Robert F. Kennedy, Sharon Tate, Janis Joplin, William Holden, Natalie Wood, John Belushi, and other lesser known cases. The history of the development of the technology and advances in criminal investigation is very interesting for me, because in my 50-year forensic career, I have witnessed many of the remarkable technological changes outlined in this book.

Chapter 1 begins with a reference to a T'ang Dynasty Magistrate, Ti Jen-Chieh, who is reputed to have used forensic evidence and logic to solve crimes. Using the facts of various cases to illustrate, the chapter goes on to describe the early history of forensic investigations and I found the discussions of some of these now-discarded theories fascinating, such as the identification of criminal types by facial structure. Subsequent chapters are well-organized into selected topics covering investigation, individual identification, weapons, knives and blunt instruments, strangulation and suffocation, and more. Each chapter starts with an informative discussion of the various elements of specific

investigative techniques, followed by factual presentation of illustrative cases, with a minimum of speculative analysis and conclusions.

Author David Owen has written for investigative-type publications since graduating from the University of Manchester, England, in 1961 with a B.Sc. in Engineering. His writing experience includes TV scripts based on fact, articles for engineering magazines, and an encyclopedia of technology and air-accident investigation.

The book is strictly factual, and easy reading for those who would like to have an introduction to the various fields of the forensic sciences, and for readers interested in the true facts of old and more current, well-known cases, some of which have been fictionalized in earlier publications.

I found, among the cases cited, some that I was either a part of the investigation or have heard and seen the scientific presentations at professional meetings, such as the annual meetings of the American Academy of Forensic Sciences (AAFS) and/or the National Association of Medical Examiners (NAME). I recall that at an AAFS meeting one year, I was a part of the speaker panel of the unique, annual scientific session called "The Last Word Society", where well-recognized forensic scientists are asked to review and give definitive thoughts or conclusions on well-known, unsolved cases. I was assigned to analyze the case of "Jack the Ripper." The author's introduction is entitled "The Trail of the Ripper" and covers this famous, and still unsolved, case.

I like *Hidden Evidence* very much for its factual, non-controversial presentation of the events with only the key issues cited. The book will be of interest to first-time readers of forensic topics, as well as long-time forensic investigators who want a synoptic, historical overview of their profession. For those interested in a quick reference to past cases with key scientific issues addressed, this is the book: an excellent mini-encyclopedia of widely discussed, high-profile cases.

I would recommend this book for every library as a quick reference to the forensic science professions. It may be of interest to science-oriented students, history majors, journalists (particularly those covering crime), and criminal investigators. *Hidden Evidence* offers testimony to the centuries of progress in forensic medicine and sciences, and criminal investigation.

Thomas T. Noguchi, M.D.

Chief Medical Examiner-Coroner (ret), and USC Professor Emeritus of Forensic Pathology

March 2000

Los Angeles, California

"Whenever you have excluded the impossible, whatever remains, however improbable, must be the truth."

Sir Arthur Conan Doyle, The Adventures of Sherlock Holmes; *The Adventure of Beryl Coronet.*

Stated differently, "The truth is out There." That assertion, made at the opening of each episode of the television series, *The X Files*, is the premise upon which forensic investigation is based. The truth is present and discoverable at every crime scene. To find it, according to Sherlock Holmes, one must follow the rules of scientific inquiry, gathering, observing, and testing data, then formulating, modifying, and rejecting hypotheses, until only one remains.

Polymerase chain reaction; Neutron activation; Microspectrophotometry; Gas chromatography; Gel electrophoresis; Mass spectrometry; Scanning electron microscopy. Today's techniques are far different from those employed by Sir Arthur Conan Doyle's fictional sleuth but the goals of police science remain the same.

The men who murdered Tsar Nicholas II and his family and servants thought their crime would never be discovered, but bones eventually came to light. Theodore Bundy was convicted by his own bitemark. DNA brought Colin Pitchfork's killing spree to an end. For the "Nightstalker," Richard Ramirez, it was a fingerprint, for Clifford Irving, a voiceprint.

Modern crime and medical examiner/coroner laboratories use a vast array of scientific specialities to exonerate the innocent and send murderers, rapists, burglars, and swindlers to jail. Bones tell stories of identity, trauma, and postmortem mutilation. The forensic anthropologist reads them. The odontologist analyzes teeth and the marks they make. People constantly exchange bits of themselves with their surroundings.

The trace evidence specialist studies hairs, fibers, pollen, paint, soil, and glass to determine who was present at a crime scene. The ballistics expert looks at tools and weapons. The biologist analyzes blood, saliva, and semen to tie perpetrators to victims or locations.

When people ask how I ended up in forensic anthropology I tell them it was accidental. In graduate school I studied archaeology and human skeletal biology, intending to focus on the ancient dead. But early in my career, when I did the occasional coroner case, I experienced an excitement I hadn't felt with prehistoric bones. The cases that came to me in body bags, or transported by sheriff's deputies, had immediacy lacking in my archaeological work. I found forensic investigation both fascinating and rewarding. I could use my science to solve a puzzle. I could provide a family with closure. I could contribute to law enforcement's effort to take criminals off the streets.

That is the purpose of forensic science, and that is what this book describes. *Hidden Evidence* takes you from crime scene to crime lab, and demonstrates how science has been used to untangle lies, both modern and historic. Commingled bones in a septic tank. Fibers in a car trunk. Paint chips on a mangled bike. Fingerprints on a bloody bat. By the use of sophisticated technology, expanded databases, and complex global linking, scientists now probe these bits and pieces, this hidden evidence, to exclude the impossible, find the truth, and sort the guilty from the innocent.

Kathy Reichs

The Trail of the Ripper...

In the late 1880s the East End of London was a grim and dangerous place to be. Grinding poverty trapped many hundreds of people in the dark and depressing jumble of the Whitechapel slums. Criminals of all kinds, from robbers and pickpockets to burglars and prostitutes, plied their trades among the poorly-lit streets, and violence was an unfortunate fact of everyday life.

One morning in November, 1888, a year in which two women had already been murdered in the area, an assistant to a local landlord called at 13 Miller's Court to collect rent owed by a twenty-four-year-old prostitute named Mary Jane Kelly. He knocked on the door and, since there was no response, peered through a broken window pane. To his horror he saw a human corpse, cut to pieces; the floor of the

room was awash with blood.

When the police arrived, they found that the woman's body had been dismantled: both breasts removed, the liver placed between the victim's feet and one hand placed in her stomach. The fireplace contained ashes of burned women's clothing.

Witnesses reported having seen the victim earlier with a man who had a mustache and was wearing a type of bowler hat known as a Derby. Two witnesses claimed they had heard a cry of "Oh, murder!" coming from the corner of Miller's Court just before four in the morning, and a neighbor had heard footsteps leaving the area some two hours later.

ABOVE 13 Miller's Court, Whitechapel, London 1888 where the mutilated body of the hapless Mary Jane Kelly was found.

LEFT Illustrated periodicals of the time fed the public appetite for details of the Ripper's murders.

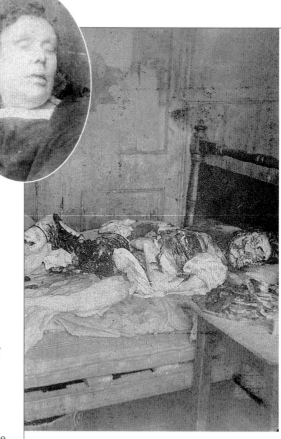

This horrific killing was the last in the series of extraordinarily savage attacks known to have been carried out by a shadowy figure nicknamed Jack the Ripper. Other brutal murders were committed during the late 1880s: some of the victims were women and some had had their throats cut, but differences in the way in which the fatal injuries had been inflicted made it unlikely that the Ripper had been involved.

In spite of the witness accounts and a tantalizing stock of forensic evidence, no credible suspect was identified in the Ripper case, though contemporary speculation was understandably rife. Over a century later, theories regarding the motives and identity of this most notorious of killers are still being published by writers, researchers and police officers. Suspects were traced and charged in connection with the later attacks, but no one with a real, provable connection to the genuine Ripper murders was ever found.

The Ripper case illustrates both the potential and the limitations of forensic science. During the twentieth century, forensic evidence has played an increasingly important role in a wide range of cases but, just as with this greatest and best-known of unsolved crimes, forensic evidence cannot find and convict the criminal unaided. It does, however, provide an additional weapon in the detective's armory; a weapon that can be used in two principal ways. It can offer clues to help detectives track down the criminal and it can help detectives prove a suspect was present at the crime scene or committed a particular act of violence. In some cases, it can even do both. By using powerful weapons such as fingerprinting and ballistics, DNA comparison, and trace-element analysis, the modern forensic scientist can uncover facts, expose crucial details, and confirm or discount theories with a certainty that would have startled previous generations.

TOP AND ABOVE RIGHT Mary Jane Kelly and Annie Chapman—both victims of the Ripper.

BELOW *The Illustrated Police News* highlighted every development.

But, spectacular as the results may be, the power of this exacting science can be fully brought to bear only once a recognizable target has been identified. Finding that target depends on solid and reliable police work.

Forensic science is not infallible. Even now there are cases where the evidence it isolates seems confusing or incomplete, or is open to more than one interpretation. Sometimes expert opinion differs over the significance of a particular finding. In other cases, techniques used to locate the tiniest traces of a particular substance have become so sensitive that a trifling weakness in laboratory hygiene or the simplest human error can lead to mistaken conclusions or inadvertent tampering with the evidence. As forensic science becomes more powerful, it must be handled with greater and more scrupulous care, if the guilty are to be convicted and the innocent exonerated.

RIGHT Fingerprints provided the first reliable proof of a person's presence at the scene of a crime and are still vital today.

BELOW Taking samples from blood-stained cloth to determine through DNA fingerprinting whether the blood was from the victim or the attacker.

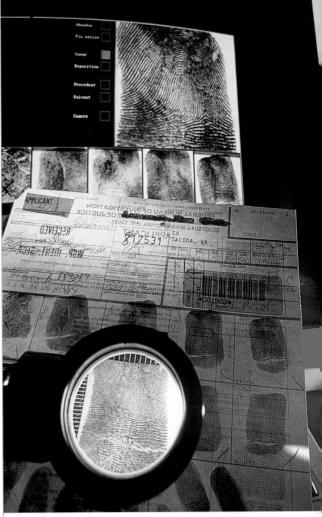

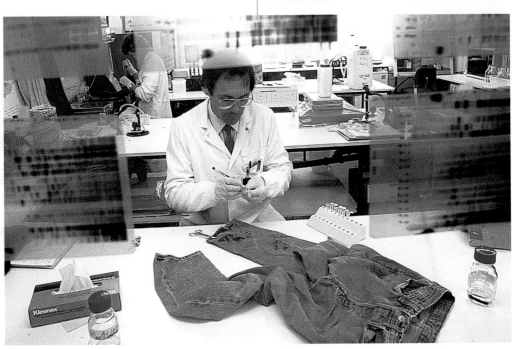

In the Beginning

ZACHARIAS IANSEN,
sive Ioannides primus Conspiciliorum inventor.

ABOVE Zacharias Jansen, inventor of the microscope. From *De vero telescopii inventora* Pierre Bond, 1655.

The dawn of forensic science as we understand it today took place in the civilization of ancient China. Documents found in Chinese archives dating back to the seventeenth century refer to a magistrate who lived a thousand years before in the remote age of the T'ang dynasty. Ti Jen-Chieh is reputed to have used both logic and forensic evidence to help solve a wide range of crimes in the late seventh century AD. Ti used a team of investigators, studied the crime scene, examined physical evidence, and interviewed witnesses and suspects. Though his methods and tools bore little resemblance to their sophisticated modern counterparts, Ti's attitude to his work and his careful investigation of the evidence would not be out of place today.

The development of forensic science owes much to the ages of scientific discovery in the sixteenth, seventeenth, and eighteenth centuries. The compound microscope was invented by Zacharias Jansen in 1590. It used a combination of lenses to produce an image much larger than that provided by the conventional magnifying glass: just two or three lenses produced a magnification of some ten times. This technique eventually allowed details of a single fingerprint to be examined

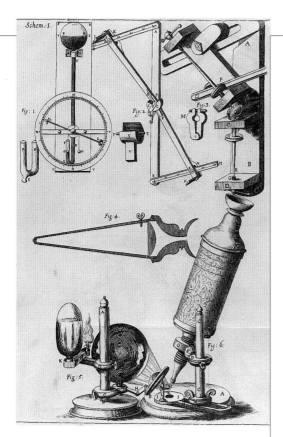

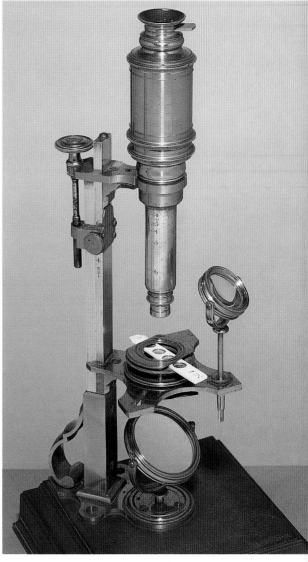

LEFT Robert Hooke's compound microscope 1665, from his book *Micrographia*.

BELOW Cuff compound microscope, 1905, photographed in the Science Museum, London.

much more closely and so compared more precisely with other prints on record cards or at a crime scene, for example.

Complex combinations of more accurately ground lenses were developed in the seventeenth century to produce a magnification of up to three hundred times. Such power enabled forensic scientists to examine hairs and fibers, blood samples, or scraps of cloth or other material, and to make informed decisions as to whether or not one sample matched another.

By the 1880s, optical microscopes with magnifications of up to two thousand times had been developed, as had other variations on the theme which were particularly useful in this field. These included the stereoscopic microscope, which has double eyepieces and double lens systems and works through prisms to provide a three-dimensional image. Stereoscopic microscopes are useful for comparing soil samples or viewing paint fragments to, for example, help identify a particular location or vehicle.

The comparison microscope, like the stereo microscope, has two lens systems, but these are combined with prisms to bring two images side by side for direct comparison, instead of superimposing them to create a third dimension. This makes it ideal for comparing the marks on two bullets to check whether or not they were fired from the same gun, or comparing samples of fabric or hair to check for a match. The comparison microscope was originally developed by Philip Gravelle and Calvin Goddard in the 1920s in New York's Bureau of Forensic Ballistics. There is now also an adaptation of the optical microscope that can be used with infrared light to show whether or not documents have been tampered with.

Photographs cannot lie?

The principle behind photographic film was first discovered in 1724 by a German inventor named Johann Heinrich Schultze. He noticed that silver salts darkened when exposed to light, at a rate that varied with the intensity of the light. Although this was the basic principle of photographic film, the image could not be fixed until 1826, when a retired French army officer named Joseph Nicéphore Niepce succeeded in focusing a beam of light on a pewter plate covered with a light-sensitive bitumen solution. In his initial experiments it took eight hours to complete the exposure, but within another thirteen years Niepce had gone into partnership with Louis Daguerre. By using a copper plate coated with silver iodide and then developing the image on the exposed plate with mercury vapor, the first photograph,

or "daguerrotype," was developed.

The method was limited to producing just one picture for each exposure, but when William Fox Talbot invented the negative, which could then be used for making any number of positive prints, the technique became much more useful. In 1850 the wet-plate enabled photographs to be taken more quickly and cheaply, and in 1871 the process became easier still with the invention of dry-plate photography. By then, photographs were being used routinely to record shots of evidence at crime scenes, details of victims and/or their injuries, and shots of subjects arrested on suspicion of committing a crime. The "Rogues' Galleries," books of full-face and profile portraits of known criminals, were important to many criminal enquiries. In 1886, New York detective Thomas Byrnes had his collection of "mug-shots" published to help the public recognize criminals who might attack or attempt to rob them.

ABOVE French physicist and inventor Joseph Neipce (1765–1833).

LEFT English photography pioneer William Henry Fox Talbot (right) at work, with device to keep sitter's head still during long exposure.

BELOW Police identification table, based upon Bertillon's system (see p. 21).

ABOVE Replica of Fox Talbot's Mousetrap, forerunner of the box camera.

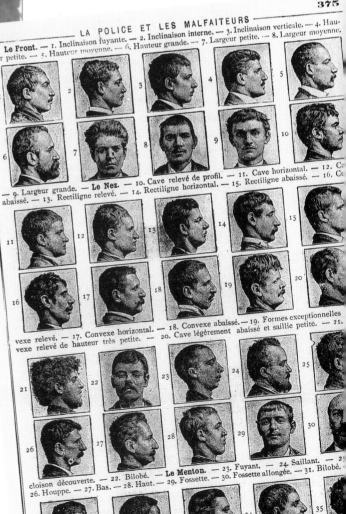

375

LA POLICE ET LES MALFAITEURS

Le Front. — 1. Inclinaison fuyante. — 2. Inclinaison interne. — 3. Inclinaison verticale. — 4. Hauteur petite. — 5. Hauteur moyenne. — 6. Hauteur grande. — 7. Largeur petite. — 8. Largeur moyenne.

9. Largeur grande. — Le Nez. — 10. Cave relevé de profil. — 11. Cave horizontal. — 12. Cave abaissé. — 13. Rectiligne relevé. — 14. Rectiligne horizontal. — 15. Rectiligne abaissé. — 16. Convexe relevé. — 17. Convexe horizontal. — 18. Convexe abaissé. — 19. Formes exceptionnelles vexe relevé de hauteur très petite. — 20. Cave légèrement abaissé et saillie petite. — 21.

cloison découverte. — 22. Bilobé. — Le Menton. — 23. Fuyant. — 24. Saillant. — 26. Houppe. — 27. Bas. — 28. Haut. — 29. Fossette. — 30. Fossette allongée. — 31. Bilobé.

40

RIGHT Exhibits from the Maybrick case, where Florence Maybrick was found guilty of poisoning her husband, Liverpool merchant James Maybrick.

Pure Poison

For hundreds if not thousands of years, poison of one sort or another has been the weapon of choice among dispassionate murderers. Avoiding the drama and mess often generated by an overtly violent death, a carefully chosen poison could be relied upon to work slowly, stealthily, and ultimately surely. With the advantage of a little background knowledge and access to the right materials, a murderer might even tailor his weapon to confuse the victim and any subsequent enquiry by using it to produce symptoms resembling those of natural killers such as heart disease or pneumonia.

But modern scientific methods make it increasingly difficult for poison to remain undetected. As long ago as 1814 Matthieu Orfila earned the title of "the father of toxicology" by publishing his book *Traité des Poisons*, which classified the common poisons favored by criminals. In 1836 another pioneer, Alfred Swaine Taylor, published a monumental textbook called *Elements of Medical Jurisprudence*, which became a classic of forensic medicine.

In October that year, English chemist James Marsh, working at the Royal Arsenal at Woolwich, south London, developed an accurate technique for revealing traces of arsenic. This poison was favored by criminals because arsenic actually already exists in small traces in the healthy human body. A victim of arsenic poisoning, however, has traces of the

ABOVE Matthieu Joseph Bonaventura Orfila, expert chemist, in 1847.

chemical in almost every part of the body as opposed to concentrations in particular organs such as the stomach or liver; these remain in the bones and hair even after death, whereas other poisons may be broken down by body chemistry. Marsh's test could reveal a trace as small as one-fiftieth of a milligram in a sample taken from the body of a victim of a suspicious death, and the principles of his technique are still in use today.

The telltale bullet

Before the mid-1830s, little could be done to link a particular weapon to a particular crime—unless of course the criminal was found at the scene clutching the still-smoking gun. In 1835, however, a policeman named Henry Goddard succeeded for the first time in tracing a bullet to the weapon that had fired it. Goddard had been a member of the Bow Street Runners, London's first police force, which had been formed in the eighteenth century as a group of "professional thieftakers."

In those days, bullets were often still molded individually by the owner of the firearm.

Goddard was called in to investigate a burglary in Southampton, and was told that the household's butler had been shot at by the intruders. He found the bullet buried in the butler's bed headboard and compared it carefully with the butler's own pistol and bullet mold. He found a raised mark on the bullet that matched a defect in the mold, proving that the shot had been fired from the butler's own weapon. Faced with the evidence, the butler admitted that it was he who had attempted to rob his employer, and that he had fired the shot in an attempt to divert suspicion from himself.

By 1869, a French investigator was able to analyze the chemical composition of a bullet found in the head of a murder victim and compare his findings with an analysis of bullets found on the chief suspect. The results proved beyond reasonable doubt that all the bullets had been molded in one batch, which strongly suggested that the suspect had made and fired the fatal bullet.

The science of ballistics developed more fully with the advent of rifled weapons and mass-produced ammunition. In 1889 Professor Alexandre Lacassagne showed that a bullet

BELOW George III (1738–1820), King of Great Britain, guarded by Bow Street Runners, forefathers of today's police force.

17

could be matched with the gun that had fired it by comparing the number of rifling grooves in the barrel with the number of grooves carved into the surface of the bullet when it was fired. The Bureau of Forensic Ballistics, founded in New York in 1923, continues to develop this increasingly sophisticated science.

The "criminal face"

Sadly, not all pioneering ideas in forensic science proved to be truly scientific. The surgeon at Toulon prison in southern France developed a theory linking habitual criminality with a particular shape of skull, and took plaster casts of the heads of notorious inmates to reinforce his ideas. In 1876 Cesare Lombroso, a forty-year-old former army surgeon and the medical superintendent of a lunatic asylum at Pesaro in northern Italy, published a treatise on criminal man, *L'Uomo Delinquente*, which claimed that his lifetime study of more than 6000 criminals had shown that they tended to possess certain well-developed physical characteristics.

In Lombroso's view, habitual criminals tended to have wide jaws, high cheekbones, long arms, and large ears (approximately square in shape), as well as an unusually narrow field of vision. He even claimed to be able to point to characteristics that were associated with particular types of criminal activity. Fire-raisers, for example, had small

heads; highwaymen had thick hair; swindlers and conmen were usually heavily built, with wide jaws and strong cheekbones, while pickpockets had usefully long hands and were often tall and dark-haired. At the time his theories were convincing enough to prompt others to invent instruments to measure these essential indications of criminal tendencies. A ball on a string was swung like a pendulum to test a suspect's field of view, for example, and a "craniometer" was developed to trace the shape of a head onto paper. But there has never been any real evidence of anything more than a random connection between physical appearance and criminal behavior.

One of Lombroso's contemporaries, an inventor named Patrizi, designed an early type of lie-detector. Called the "volumetric glove," the device was made of gutta-percha, a tough, grayish-black plastic substance from the latex of various Malayan trees. It was designed to fit over the hand and be tightly sealed at the wrist. The glove was then filled with air and connected to a tube linked to an apparatus for recording changes in pressure caused by the pulse in the veins of the hand. When questions were put to the suspect, an increase in emotional tension was supposedly shown by an increase in the blood flow to the hand, and a consequent increase in the pressure changes caused by the pulse. Sadly, the glove was no more reliable than the "criminal face" as an indicator of criminal tendencies.

OPPOSITE Bertillon's attempts to find a way of recording individual facial details depended on recording these measurements very accurately. Here a 1907 subject is photographed under controlled studio conditions for his details to be recorded (see p. 21).

HIDDEN
EVIDENCE

Tests for poisons

Forensic scientists faced with a victim of poisoning have a daunting array of possible agents to search for at autopsy. The procedure often starts with samples of the victim's blood, urine, or specific tissues being dissolved in an acidified or alkaline solution. Acidified water is used when looking for evidence of acidic drugs such as ASA or barbiturates, which can be extracted from the solution using organic solvents such as chloroform.

A screening test can check quite rapidly for a wide range of drugs or poisons. Complicated

RIGHT Forensic drug testing. High pressure liquid chromatography is used to identify drugs in a forensic laboratory.

BELOW A gas chromatography machine connected to a mass spectrometer in a forensic laboratory. A sample injection robot transfers samples from small vials to the chromatography machine where they are evaporated and separated according to molecular weight. The spectrometer identifies the smallest traces of individual chemicals as they emerge from the chromatography tube.

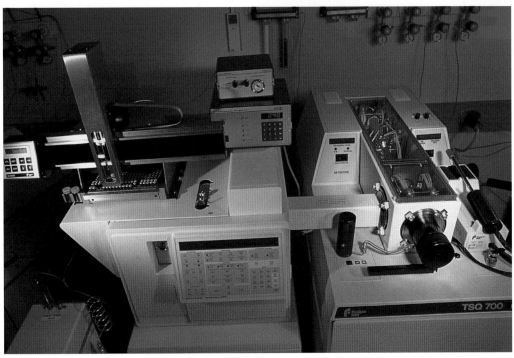

BELOW Forensic narcotic tests: a selection of vials used by police officers at the scene of a crime to test for illegal narcotics. Each vial is marked with the narcotic it can identify (from left; opiates and amphetamines; cannabis; LSD; cocaine). During a test the top of the vial is broken off and a sample of the drug inserted into the vial using a spatula. A positive result will be indicated by the clear crystals inside the vial changing to the color indicated on the vial.

mixtures can be broken down into their constituent parts using a technique called gas chromatography. A liquid sample is introduced into a heated injection port where it is vaporized and carried on a stream of gas through a liquid-filled column. The various constituents of the mixture travel at unequal speeds through the liquid column, and emerge at different times. By placing a detector at the end of the column, the individual constituents are revealed as peaks on a moving strip chart. Each of the peaks can be identified as a particular substance by comparing the strip chart with other reference charts, and the height of each peak shows the amount of each particular substance in the sample.

Forensic analysts use thin-layer chromatography as a screening test to identify types of drugs. This works in a similar way except that it places the sample on a thin vertical film of silica gel or aluminum oxide. The sample is then split into its different constituents by a liquid solvent which rises up the surface of the film by capillary action, attracting some substances more strongly than others and carrying them further. When the process is finished, the plate carrying the vertical film is placed under ultraviolet light, which shows the different constituents of the mixture as dark or fluorescent spots. Alternatively a chemical agent can be used that reacts differently with each constituent, causing them to reveal themselves as different-colored spots.

Recently, forensic laboratories have been turning to immuno-assay techniques to test samples for very small amounts of drugs or poisons. This involves the development of antibodies that react with the substances being looked for. First, the drug in question is combined with a protein and the compound injected into the bloodstream of an animal. This stimulates the animal to produce antibodies, which are extracted from a blood sample, then added to the test sample. If the drug in question is present in the test sample, the antibodies from the animal's blood will be seen to react with it.

Confirmation tests usually involve a combination of gas chromatography and mass spectrometry. As each different component from the sample mixture emerges from the chromatography column, it enters into a mass spectrometer where it is bombarded by a stream of high-energy electrons. These electrons then cause the component to break up, producing a different but characteristic spectrum for each individual substance present.

Aunt Thally

The death of an eighty-seven-year-old woman named Christina Mickelson in Sydney, Australia, in 1947 seemed a natural enough occurrence. When family friend Angeline Thomas died not long afterward this too seemed reasonable, given that the lady was also in her eighties. But the death of a much younger relative, sixty-year-old John Lundberg, a year later was more suspicious. Lundberg's hair had fallen out before his death, which made it all the more alarming when another member of the family, Mary Ann Mickelson, fell ill with similar symptoms, and finally she too died.

One factor common to all four deaths was the presence of Caroline Grills, the sixty-three-year-old stepdaughter-in-law of the first victim. Grills, who had married Mrs. Mickelson's stepson nearly forty years earlier, had nursed the old lady through her final illness. When Angeline Thomas fell ill, Grills had helped care for her too, preparing endless cups of tea to lift the invalid's spirits. She had also been there to minister to John Lundberg and Mary Ann Mickelson and, one after another, her patients' conditions had all deteriorated until eventually they died.

By 1948, the mystery sickness had begun to threaten the lives of John Lundberg's widow and daughter, both of whose conditions were worsening in spite of Caroline Grills' attentive care. Both women were losing their hair and complained of a heavy lassitude and difficulty in moving their limbs. Eventually a suspicious relative alerted the local police, who removed one of the cups of tea prepared for the suffering women and subjected it to forensic analysis. The fact that the victims' hair had fallen out during their illness suggested the presence of thallium as a poison. The laboratory checked by using the Reinsch test, which involves adding the suspect material to a solution of hydrochloric acid. A copper strip is dipped into the resulting mixture, and any metallic deposit forming on it indicates the presence of a heavy metal such as arsenic, antimony, or thallium. The specific identity of the contamination is then confirmed by further analysis.

Thallium was found to have been added to the tea. Discovery was made in time to save the lives of Mrs. Lundberg and her daughter, athough Mrs. Lundberg lost her sight as a result of the poison absorbed into her system.

Caroline Grills was tried and found guilty of the attempted murder of Mrs. Lundberg. She was sentenced to life imprisonment and, bizarrely, became popular among the other inmates who came to know her simply as "Aunt Thally."

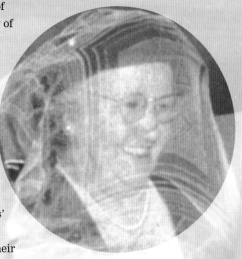

BACKGROUND A picture of Caroline Grills, who used thallium to poison her victims.

Dr. Hawley Harvey Crippen

ABOVE Dr Bernard Spilsbury in the pathology laboratory at St Bartholomew's Hospital, London.

BELOW Hilldrop Crescent in North London, taken in August 1910.

D r. Hawley Harvey Crippen was an American-born dentist. He was married to a former music-hall singer whose stage name was Belle Elmore. After Mrs. Crippen disappeared early in 1910, neighbors' suspicions were aroused by Crippin's mistress, Ethel le Neve, who was seen wearing Mrs. Crippen's jewelry. Crippen and le Neve fled to Antwerp in Belgium whereupon, on July 13, police searched the Crippens' home at Hilldrop Crescent in north London, and found the mutilated body of a woman, but no proof of her identity.

British pathologist Dr. Bernard Spilsbury carried out an autopsy and was able to prove the existence of an appendectomy scar which helped to identify the body as definitely that of Mrs. Crippen. He also found traces of hyoscine, which showed that the woman had been deliberately poisoned. Because hyoscine produced symptoms similar to heart failure, and because it was available to medical practitioners for use in small doses as a treatment for anxiety and travel sickness, suspicion was cast on Dr. Crippen and police began a search for him and his mistress.

By this time, the couple were crossing the Atlantic on the steamship *Montrose*, posing as "Mr. Robinson and son." The captain became suspicious of their affectionate behavior and sent a wireless message to England. Chief Inspector Dew of Scotland Yard responded, boarding a steamer that reached

Canada before the *Montrose* was due to land. As Crippen's ship approached the Canadian coast, Dew went to meet it, disguised as a pilot. He subsequently arrested the couple and they were taken back to England for trial. Crippen, perhaps the first criminal to be caught as a result of a wireless message, was hanged later that year. Le Neve was tried as an accessory, but was later acquitted after her defense showed she had been unaware of the murder.

ABOVE Dr. Crippen walking down the gangway, his arm clasped by a detective, on their return to England.

BELOW Dr. Crippen and Ethel Le Neve during their trial at Bow Street.

ARRESTATION DU DOCTEUR CRIPPEN ET DE MISS LE NEVE SUR LE PONT DU «MONTROSE»

ABOVE The moment of the arrest on board the *Montrose* August 14, 1910, as depicted in the French magazine *Le Petit Journal*.

Arthur Warren Waite

POISONER AND THE ORDER HE SIGNED FOR PROCURING SERVANT'S TESTIMONY.

DR. ARTHUR WARREN WAITE

FROM PHOTOGRAPH MADE LAST DECEMBER

ORDER SIGNED by DR. WAITE For PROCURING DORA HELLIER'S TESTIMONY

Most poisons can be revealed by careful forensic analysis, but some murderers have tried to avoid suspicion by using genuine diseases to kill their victims. Dr. Arthur Warren Waite was a New York dentist who succeeded in poisoning his mother-in-law by lacing her food with a mixture of influenza and diphtheria germs. She died in January 1916. Dr. Waite then set to work on John Peck, his father-in-law, using in addition a nasal spray contaminated with tuberculosis germs. Though Peck proved more resistant to infection than his late wife, he died just two months after her. Among the tests conducted at Peck's autopsy was the standard test for arsenic poisoning, which had been developed by London chemist James Marsh eighty years earlier. Specimens of body tissue or stomach contents are placed on a zinc plate and sulfuric acid is poured onto the sample. Any arsenic is turned into a gaseous compound of arsenic and hydrogen, which passes along a heated tube to a cold section where arsenious oxide collects. In this case, the resulting white crystals of arsenious oxide showed that the impatient Dr. Waite had indeed added this more certain poison to his armory, and as a result he was convicted of his father-in-law's murder.

ABOVE A picture of Dr. Waite and the order he signed for procuring his servant's testimony.

OPPOSITE A newspaper report about the arrest of Dr. Waite, showing the victims. Mr. and Mrs. Peck, and below, their children, one of whom was the wife of Dr. Waite.

WAITE, IN DRUG STUPOR, UNDER ARREST, CHARGED WITH POISONING PECK.

POISONED MILLIONAIRE, DEAD WIFE, AND HEIRS

MRS. JOHN E. PECK

JOHN E. PECK

MRS. ARTHUR W. WAITE

PERCY PECK

Detective Finds Dentist Unconscious in Riverside Apartment —In Lucid Moment Asks Doctor to Use Stomach Pump and Says He Took "Plenty" to Induce Sleep—Had Medical Book With Information About Poisons—Many Packages of Strong Chemicals in Pockets—Servant Tells Grand Jury She Saw Employer Pour "Medicine" in Aged Father-in-Law's Soup and Tea Two Nights Before Latter's Death.

District Attorney Swann at 10 o'clock yesterday morning ordered the arrest of Dr. Arthur Warren Waite, in whose apartment in the Colosseum, No. 435 Riverside Drive, John E. Peck, a millionaire druggist of Grand Rapids, Mich., died on March 12.

The District Attorney's action followed hard upon the clue he found in the publication in The World of the suggestion of Miss Catherine Peck, a sister of the dead man, that he might have "gone to Dr. Waite's study, got the bottle of arsenic there, and taken a dose of it by mistake."

Physically, at least, Dr. Waite was not put under arrest, for Detective Cunniff of the District Attorney's staff found him deeply under the influence of drugs which he had taken, he said in intervals of coherence, at 11 o'clock Wednesday morning in an effort to induce sleep.

Waite continued violently ill at intervals throughout the day, but there was reason to believe that he would have recovered sufficiently by this morning to be placed actually under arrest and arraigned on a charge of homicide in connection with the death of Mr. Peck, whose son-in-law he was, and whose wife had died six weeks earlier, almost to the hour, in the Waite apartment.

Information on Poisons Marked in Books Found in Rooms

Mr. Swann found in the apartment yesterday, in the course of a two and one-half hours examination of it, several works on medical and chemical subjects. One of these was Woods on therapeutics and pharmacology. Between pages 211 and 212 was found a book mark, a yellowed strip of paper, that seemed to have been in place for a long time. On these pages the topic under discussion was "Arsenic: Effects on the System."

Between pages 158 and 159 was another mark, indicating a discussion of veratria (an organic alkali) and white hellebore. Between pages 662 and 663 there was still another mark, indicating a discussion of nauseating and depressive expectorant.

"These may be old references," said the District Attorney. "I don't say that they have any significance."

Mr. Swann, however, took the volume to his office with him.

Meantime the Grand Jury, sitting under Judge Nott of the Court of General Sessions, began an inquiry into the death of Mr. Peck. Two witnesses had been heard when it adjourned at 1.30 o'clock until 11 this morning—Dora Hillier, the West Indian servant employed by the Waites, and Dr. Jacob Cornell of Raritan, N. J., an intimate of Mr. Peck and, it is now believed, the author of the telegram signed "K. Adams," which prevented the cremation of the body of Mr. Peck and brought about the autopsies which revealed the presence of arsenic.

Servant Tells Strong Story.

had seen Dr. Waite put "medicine" in soup and tea served to Mr. Peck one evening, about two days before he died. Dr. Cornell similarly told of having found Mr. Peck in apparently good health less than twelve hours before he died, and of finding himself a "seemingly unwelcome" guest when he visited the Waite apartment shortly afterward.

Witnesses called from Grand Rapids for appearance before the Grand Jury are on their way East, and may be heard to-morrow. Mr. and Mrs. Warren W. Waite, father and mother of the young dentist, started for this city last night. Assistant District Attorney F. X. Mancuso, who has been in Michigan with Dr. Otto H Schultze, the District Attorney's pathologist, believes he has established facts of the utmost importance in the past three days. He telegraphed to his chief last night an enthusiastic account of his work, concluding:

"Check up bank accounts and hold up deposits."

Mr. Swann had already taken this action, impounding deposits Dr. Waite carried in a Fifth Avenue bank and the contents of a box in a safe deposit vault in East Fourteenth Street. The World established during the day that Dr. Waite had received from Miss Peck, his wife's aunt, considerably more than the $40,000 in cash of which she told Wednesday. Securities whose face value would bring the total close to $100,000 were also added to this.

Other Woman Still Unknown.

Only one aspect of the life of Dr.

RECORDS OF BRITISH CRUISER AS FLOTSAM.

First Believed That Cumberland Had Been Sunk—No Dates Beyond 1908.

(Special to The World.)

NORFOLK, Va., March 23.—There was a sensation here to-day when members of the Coast Guard at Chicomiconclo, N. C., reported that they had picked up the log books of the British cruiser Cumberland, washed ashore on the beach.

The excitement considerably subsided when it was discovered that of the six books picked up, not one carried an entry later than 1908. They were, moreover, not the ship's logs, but apparently some of the records of the engineer's force.

Many fishermen were ready to swear they had heard heavy firing at sea recently.

Communication with the British Embassy at Washington suggested the explanation that the books were discarded records.

FLETCHER ON WAY TO TALK TO LANSING.

PANAMA, March 23.—Henry P. Fletcher, the new American Ambassador to Mexico, passed through here to-day and sailed this afternoon on the steamer Corrillo for New York on his way to Washington from his former post at Santiago, Chili.

Mr. Fletcher said he was not prepared to discuss the problems confronting him in Mexico, because he was not possessed of information on the situation. He was going to Washington, he added, to receive instructions from Secretary of State Lansing and familiarize himself thoroughly with the conditions and with what was expected of him.

The Hub Clothiers' Final Sale.

The "HUB," Broadway at Barclay St. (Opp. Woolworth Building). Specially priced for to-day & Saturday, the entire balance of our $10 & $12 Men's Young

MRS. ARTHUR W. WAITE

PERCY

Knives and Blunt Instruments

ABOVE Some of the weapons used by "Yorkshire Ripper" Peter Sutcliffe.

With the decline in the general availability of poisons, and the increasing probability of their use being revealed by autopsy evidence, modern criminals tend to use other weapons to achieve their ends. In the U.S., where firearms and ammunition are relatively easy to obtain, a high proportion of woundings and murders involve gunshot wounds (*see* Chapter Eight). Nevertheless, use of a firearm often implies a degree of premeditation and can also provide evidence allowing forensic scientists to tie the weapon, and ultimately the user, to the murder. In less carefully planned attacks, cruder weapons are used, ranging from a stiletto, a switchblade, or kitchen knife, to the nearest heavy object able to inflict a sufficiently damaging wound—be it a wrench, a lamp, or a lump of wood. It is the job of the forensic scientist either to show that a particular weapon was the one used in a given case or, in cases where the weapon has not been found, to give a description of the weapon based on the victim's injuries to assist investigators in their search for evidence.

Evidence on the victim

In cases where a murder victim has been battered to death with a blunt instrument, the fatal blows are usually delivered to the head, and it is relatively unusual for one single blow to achieve the criminal's aim. A series of blows is usually sustained, each of which can cause ragged lacerations where scraps of tissue and blood vessels are driven into the surface of the underlying bones.

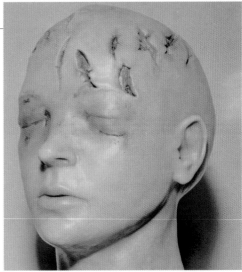

ABOVE A medical model of the head of Mrs. Marilyn Sheppard showing the horrific injuries she received. Her husband, Dr. Sam Sheppard, was found guilty of her murder in 1954, but was acquitted and released in 1966.

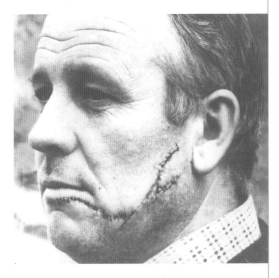

ABOVE Graham Backhouse slashed his own cheek after killing a neighbor, claiming he had been attacked and had shot back in self-defence.

The victim's head may show depression fractures where the bones of the skull were driven into the brain tissues, causing death by compression of the brain. In such cases, the shape of the fractured area may reveal something of the shape of the weapon used. The site of the fracture area, seen in the context of the victim's probable position when the blows were delivered, can also indicate the type of blow delivered, and even the relative height and strength of the attacker. There may be no discernible depression fractures, however, if the fatal injuries were caused by rupture of the blood vessels beneath the skull.

Sometimes the fatal injuries are only part of the evidence found on the victim's body. If the attack was prolonged, or a physical struggle preceded the murder, patterns of bruising can give an indication of what happened.

Bruises are caused by the breaking of small blood vessels beneath the skin. They might be caused by the attacker's fists, feet, or weapons, or by the victim falling against hard or sharp objects at the scene of the attack. Bruises can show forensic experts something of the order in which the attack progressed, and where and how the fatal blow was struck. Examination can also reveal whether the rupture of the blood vessels happened before or after death. In cases where the bruising was inflicted before death, a sample of the blood found beneath the skin at the site of the bruise usually shows a higher-than-normal white-cell count, because the body's normal reactions to an injury started to function immediately after the injury was sustained. If the bruise was inflicted after death, this process would not normally have progressed to the same extent.

Children who have been battered by their parents or caretakers are often too young or too frightened to give evidence regarding the nature of their injuries. Because bruises heal in a series of stages over several days or weeks, the injuries themselves can indicate that either a single incident or a series of repeated attacks was responsible.

For example, a fresh bruise usually appears purple or red in color, depending on the depth and size of the injury. Chemical changes that affect the blood that leaks into the tissues cause the bruise to change to brown, and then to green, and finally to yellow before the signs slowly fade. Consequently, a victim showing fresh reddish-purple bruises, together with others that are brown, and others that are greenish-yellow, is likely to have been attacked on at least three separate occasions.

Knife Wounds

In countries where gun-control laws are tightly enforced, murders with knives are usually the most common type of killing. Even in the U.S., the number of knife murders is second only to the number of those involving guns. Though there is as yet no foolproof technique for positively linking an individual knife to an individual victim, as there is with guns and bullets (see Chapter Eight), knife murders do offer forensic experts some useful clues to help in their search for the perpetrator.

Knife wounds are almost always inflicted during close-range attacks. In the case of incised wounds, where the attacker makes a series of slashing moves, cuts to the victim's arms and hands often show where he or she has instinctively tried to intercept the blows in an attempt at self-defense. Struggles of this kind usually leave the attacker spattered or

LEFT AND ABOVE A Turkish debtor fatally stabs his creditor in broad daylight. The slaying was captured by a passing journalist.

ABOVE Peter Sutcliffe, the "Yorkshire Ripper."

Careful inspection of a stab wound can reveal useful details of the knife used. Though information on the width of the blade is often unreliable, because the knife may have been moved within the body after the initial stab, the weapon must have been at least as long as the depth of the resulting wound. A skilled anthropologist can often tell whether the wound was made by a double-edged blade or by a blade that has only a single sharp edge.

Not all stab wounds are caused by knives, of course. A victim could be stabbed with a chisel, a screwdriver, or a pair of scissors, for example. An elaborate technique is sometimes used to produce a cast of the wound, to give more accurate evidence of the shape and form of the

ABOVE In the case of one murdered woman, a pathologist found a knife blade tip in a neck wound, which fitted the broken blade of a penknife found in the pants pocket of her husband, the accused.

even drenched in the victim's blood: such bloodstains, if found, offer proof positive of the attacker's presence at the assault.

Forensic experts recognize another basic type of knife wound. Stab wounds are inflicted when the knife blade is pushed into the body, causing damage to the body's vital organs and producing internal bleeding. In these cases there may be relatively little external bleeding and, if the knife is removed, the wound can shrink so as to appear less obvious than an incised wound.

Stab wounds are usually fatal only when they are inflicted with a sufficiently long blade to the chest or abdomen. In attacks to the chest, blows are usually delivered upward so the knife tends to penetrate the chest wall between the ribs. A downward blow to the chest can result in the knife blade glancing off each of the ribs in turn, preventing it from entering deeply enough to inflict fatal damage to the victim.

weapon. This involves dissecting layer by layer the part of the victim's body that contains the wound, enabling a three-dimensional representation to be built up. In at least one case the victim's chest, and the fatal wound, were preserved in formalin after the autopsy. The murder weapon was subsequently found and presented as evidence; prosecutors were able to demonstrate in court that the shape of the weapon matched that of the wound.

Fatal incised wounds are usually those delivered to the body's most unprotected area—where the arteries supplying blood to the brain are exposed around the victim's neck. In reality, it is surprisingly difficult for an attacker to cut a victim's throat in the course of an equal struggle. If the throat has been cut, there is often evidence that the victim was held down, tied up or rendered unconscious before the fatal injury was sustained.

BELOW Bodies being recovered from a murder scene.

Homicide—or suicide?

Relatively few suicides use knives, though cases do occur, and forensic scientists have to recognize the signs that differentiate suicide and murder victims. In general, suicides who use knives target one of three sites on the body: they attempt to cut the throat, or to stab themselves in the chest or stomach.

In cases where a suicide stabs him- or herself through the heart or stomach, there are usually just one or two deliberate stabs. In most cases, clothing has been removed over the target area and the wound is located within the victim's easy reach to allow the blow to be delivered with sufficient force. In cases where there are multiple stab wounds over a wider area of the body, and where these are wholly or partly delivered through the clothing, then homicide is the more likely cause.

Where death has resulted from the severing of major blood vessels to the neck, the site of the cut and its appearance reveal a great deal

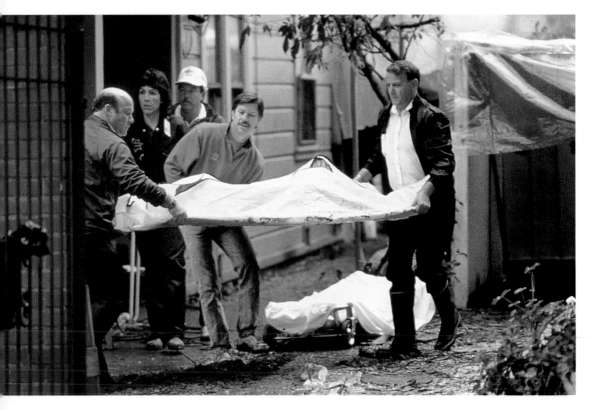

about how it was inflicted. A right-handed suicide usually inflicts a gash that starts high on the left side of the neck, sweeps across the throat and finishes lower down on the right side. A left-handed suicide commonly operates in the other direction, starting high up on the right side of the neck and sweeping across to finish low down on the left side.

Two further signs distinguish suicides from victims attacked by other parties. In a suicide where the throat is cut, there is often evidence of one or two shallower gashes caused by "trial attempts" made while the person built up sufficient determination to deliver the final, lethal cut. There is also a tendency for the suicide to raise the head at the moment of impact, intending to expose the neck arteries. In fact this can often defeat the object, because such action moves the blood vessels back to a position where they are at least partly shielded by the windpipe. Sometimes the attempt fails completely, or death results from suffocation when blood from the surrounding tissues enters the windpipe and prevents the victim from breathing.

Where the throat has been cut by an attacker, a fatal wound inflicted at one side of the neck often indicates whether the attacker was left- or right-handed or whether the blow was struck from in front of the victim or from behind. In addition, unless the victim was asleep or restrained at the time of the attack, there is usually evidence of defensive wounds to the hands, as well as to the arms, which is proof positive that the crime was homicidal rather than suicidal.

Even in cases where the criminal tries to disguise murder to look like suicide, telltale details can give the game away. In one case in England, a murderer placed a knife in his victim's hand, having deliberately inflicted cuts to his own body, and claimed he had shot his victim in self-defense. When checked by forensic experts the evidence revealed that the victim could not have continued to hold the knife after suffering the shock of a shotgun

ABOVE Mummified head of *Lindow Man*, dated between 20 and 130 AD, who met a violent end, being struck on the head and garroted, a method of strangling.

blast to the chest unless rigor mortis had set in immediately, and there was no evidence of this.

Furthermore, the nature of the wounds on the murderer's body was inconsistent with his story: they appeared to have been made while he was standing fairly still and there were no defensive wounds on his arms or hands to support his claim that he had tried to fend off the victim's attack. Another detail that cast suspicion on his story involved the state of the dead man's hand in which the knife was found. The palm was soaked in blood where the victim had clutched the massive wound to his chest. Had he actually been attacking with the knife when the shot was fired, the hand would not have been soaked in blood unless he had dropped the knife to clutch his wound.

Jeffrey MacDonald

ABOVE U.S. Army Captain Jeffrey MacDonald.

BELOW A military policeman stands guard as a crime lab technician works inside the MacDonald home.

Jeffrey MacDonald was a captain in the U.S. Army, living with his wife and two young daughters at Fort Bragg in North Carolina. Military police responding to an emergency telephone call in the small hours of the morning found the wife and daughters dead from numerous stab wounds. MacDonald was alive, and claimed he had been stabbed and knocked unconscious by three men and a woman: all "hippies," and apparently acting under the influence of drugs. He explained how he had warded off their frenzied blows by wrapping his blue pajama jacket around his hands, and how, after the attackers fled, he had first tried to revive his daughters with mouth-to-mouth resuscitation, then placed the jacket over his dead wife's body.

MacDonald gave detailed descriptions of all four attackers, but no evidence of their presence could be found. Officers were suspicious of MacDonald's story because the room had been in darkness at the time of the attack, and MacDonald had very poor eyesight. He needed glasses to read and to drive, so without them, his vision would have been blurred. When a forensic team searched the scene, they found blue fibers from his pajama jacket beneath his wife's body, in the children's bedrooms, and under the fingernail of one of the victims. But none was found in the living room where MacDonald claimed to have been fighting for his life, and where there was in fact very little disorder. The bloodstains in the different rooms were all identified, and

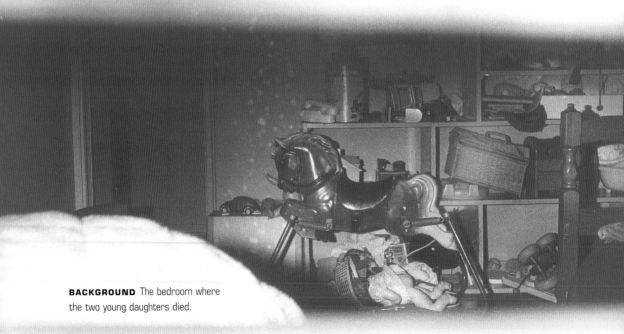

BACKGROUND The bedroom where the two young daughters died.

MacDonald's blood was found in the kitchen, in the bathroom, and on a pair of eyeglasses. No traces were found in the living room where he claimed to have been stabbed, or on either of the telephones he had used to call the police.

Nevertheless, many pieces of evidence had been lost by the time his trial was due, and charges were dropped. But when MacDonald subsequently appeared on a television chat show, his callous attitude and the flippant remarks he made regarding his family's tragic deaths revived suspicions as to his part in the drama, and his pajama jacket was sent to the FBI laboratory in Washington D.C. for analysis. Investigators found that all forty-eight holes said to have been made by the attackers' ice pick were smooth and round, rather as if the jacket had been held still while the holes had been made. There was also a large stain of Mrs. MacDonald's blood on both sides of a tear said to have been made during the attack. This suggested that the stain had been produced before the jacket was torn, although MacDonald claimed to have laid the jacket across his wife's body only after the attack was over and he had found her dead.

Finally in 1979 MacDonald was tried for the murders of his wife and children. During the course of the trial, forensic examiners demonstrated a simulated attack in the courtroom with an ice-pick and a pajama jacket. They showed that the pattern of cuts made in the pajama jacket was not consistent with the pattern of cuts that would have been made had the incident unfolded as MacDonald originally claimed. As a result, MacDonald was found guilty and ordered to serve three consecutive life sentences. A succession of appeals, started in October 1997, are still going on.

ABOVE MacDonald pictured on the day before he was accused of killing his pregnant wife and his children.

LEFT Artist's sketch shown at the preliminary hearing depicting a woman described by MacDonald as involved in the murders of his wife and children.

Strangulation and Suffocation

RIGHT Sketch of Colonel Edward Marcus Despart at New Surrey Gaol just before his hanging.

If an attacker has neither a gun nor a knife, and there is no object on hand that is hard and heavy enough to batter the victim with, a murderer may opt for strangulation or suffocation. Strangulation may be with a cord, a rope, or a length of wire, or it may be by the murderer's own hands. Suffocation may be due to a pillow or plastic bag over the face or by a weight (such as the murderer's body) being pressed on the chest of the victim making

breathing impossible. But forensic examination of the scene and body can still reveal exactly how the victim died, sometimes in spite of the criminal's best efforts to cover his or her tracks or to conceal the fact that a crime has taken place at all.

Accidental suffocation happens when the victim is starved of air because of where he or she happens to be, rather than because of the actions of an assailant. If a child happens to

find an abandoned refrigerator, for example, and accidentally becomes trapped inside, then unless he or she is rescued in time, the lack of oxygen will result in unconsciousness and eventually death. This would be classed as an accidental suffocation. On the other hand, if a kidnap victim is left concealed in a confined space and dies of suffocation, the case would be a criminal death, even if it was due to error rather than deliberate intention.

Victims can also be accidentally suffocated by what is described as crush asphyxia. If a

ABOVE The Hillsborough disaster at a soccer stadium in Sheffield, England, where stampeding crowds caused deaths from crush asphyxia.

victim is trapped in a crowd, or by a fall in a mine or quarry, or by falling concrete in an earthquake, the weight of other people or of the debris may bear so heavily on the chest that breathing is impossible. In such cases there are usually signs of hemorrhaging from the head and chest and around the eyeballs, which are often full of excess fluid.

Examining the clues

Death by asphyxiation results from air being prevented from reaching the lungs.

A victim of strangling often dies because the supply of blood and oxygen to the brain is cut off.

Excess pressure on the vagus nerve during strangulation can cause it to send a signal to the brain ordering the heart to stop beating.

Separation of the vertebrae can rupture blood and tear the spinal cord, causing instant death.

Smothering and "Burking"

When a victim dies because breathing is physically impossible, rather than owing to lack of oxygen, the cause of death is usually described as smothering. Victims can be smothered accidentally, as in cases where an unsupervised child puts a plastic bag over his or her head and cuts off the air supply. Sometimes—but not always—the influence of drink or drugs is involved in adult cases: people die from becoming entangled in clothing or bedding; from choking on food or vomit, or in cases of auto-erotic asphyxiation.

Nevertheless, some smothering cases occur as a result of a deliberate assault. Criminals sometimes choose the method in the hope that the absence of obvious injuries like bruising or knife wounds will lead investigators to

ABOVE The house at Tanner's Close in Edinburgh where Burke and Hare carried out their killings.

conclude that the victim suffered a seizure or heart attack. The notorious nineteenth-century "bodysnatchers" Burke and Hare made a living by murdering victims to sell their bodies to the anatomy departments of teaching hospitals in Edinburgh, Scotland. The murderers needed the bodies to be in good condition and have no external injuries. They therefore perfected a method of killing that involved their kneeling on the victim's chest and using their hands to close off the nose and mouth, a technique which ever since has been known to criminals and the police as "Burking."

LEFT Burke and Hare's common-law wives helped drug the victims with whisky before they were suffocated.

BELOW Burke and Hare soffocating one of their victims, to sell the corpse for medical dissection.

ABOVE Harry Dobkin killed his estranged wife Rachel (top) and hid her dismembered body in a bomb-damaged chapel in wartime London.

Manual strangulation

Where a victim has been strangled by the assailant's hands, there are two main causes of death. The pressure of the hands around the throat not only prevents the victim from breathing, but can also cut off the blood supply to the brain. As a result, a determined attack may render the victim unconscious— preventing any further resistance—before death occurs.

To a forensic scientist, the body of a victim of manual strangulation shows clear signs of what has happened. In order to cut off both respiration and blood circulation, the attacker has to apply enough force to cause bruising of the victim's neck and throat. The bruises are brought about by the pressure of the thumbs and fingertips and are usually approximately circular in shape and around half an inch in diameter. Curved marks may also be caused by

fingernails tearing into the victim's skin.

Other signs result from the victim's physical reaction to the strangulation. They may include the trapping of the tongue between the teeth, causing bite marks and bruising of the tissues. There may also be bruising of the surrounding area including the lining of the larynx, the voice box, and the floor of the mouth. As with any death from strangulation, it is likely that the hyoid bone, a curved bone at the base of the tongue, will have been broken, and if the attacker has used a great deal of force there may also be fractures of the cartilage of the windpipe and larynx. Another telltale sign of strangulation is the presence of pinpoint hemorrhages around the eyes.

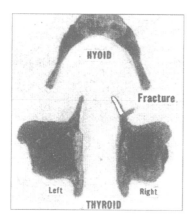

ABOVE Pathologist Keith Simpson found damage to the larynx that showed Rachel Dobkin had been strangled.

A fall—or a push?

The most obvious external evidence found on the body of a hanging victim is usually caused by the rope itself. The marks made on the victim differ according to the type of noose used. If the rope is tied as a running noose, the weight of the body tightens the rope to the extent that it presses an almost horizontal groove around the neck. With a fixed noose, on the other hand, there is enough slack for the rope from which the victim is hanging to distort the noose by pulling it upward at an angle, making a mark like an inverted letter V on the victim's neck. Because a fixed noose pulls to one side, the victim's head often tilts away from the vertical part of the rope, so the rope mark may not run right around the neck.

Whether the hanging was self-inflicted or the work of a murderer, the victim usually shows the effects of asphyxia. When the oxygen supply to the blood fails, the deoxygenated blood turns a characteristic blue color that can be seen in a blueness of the lips and tongue. The tongue often protrudes between the lips, the pupils of the eyes are usually dilated, and because the blood supply to the head is cut off by the rope, the face is literally deathly pale.

Since these effects can also be caused by straightforward strangulation, forensic examiners pay particularly close attention to the neck of the victim to search for any bruising or other injuries that would not have

OPPOSITE The beam where the murdered wife was supposed to have hanged herself in the 1925 case.

BELOW Michael Hutchence, leader of the musical group INXS, who allegedly committed suicide by hanging in 1997.

been caused by a noose. A search of the scene of the hanging may also reveal inconsistencies if there has been a deliberate attempt to confuse the picture. A genuine suicide, for example, found hanging clear of the ground, would have used a ladder or a chair to stand on while putting on the noose, and this would be found at the scene.

One murderer who tried to fake his wife's suicide in southern England in 1925 overlooked a most basic detail. He claimed to have found his wife hanging after she had committed suicide, and explained that he had cut down her body before calling the police. Forensic examiners checked the beam from which the rope was supposed to have hung and found it covered in dust with no sign of disturbance by a rope or anything else.

Strangulation by ligature

If a victim is strangled by a ligature, such as rope or cord, being pulled tight around the neck, forensic examiners will find marks on the neck revealing the cause of death. These

usually appear as a more or less horizontal groove, which is situated lower down the neck than it would be had the victim been hanged, since in that case the body falls into the ligature under gravity.

Some deductions about the type of ligature used can be made from the appearance of the marks. A deep and narrow mark indicates some form of wire, cord, or cable was used, while a broader, shallower scar is more likely to have been caused by a tie, a belt, pantihose or a scarf, for example. Generally speaking the softer the material, the less obvious the mark at first sight, but if enough force has been applied to cause the victim's death, then some kind of discernible mark is bound to be present.

If the ligature is found at the scene, it can become vital evidence in its own right. The material used may have a link with the victim or, more importantly, with the attacker. Even the way in which the ligature is used can provide clues. Some killers simply loop the ends around one another and pull, in the manner of the Thug ritual stranglers of ancient India; others use a knot of some kind. The ligature used by the infamous Boston

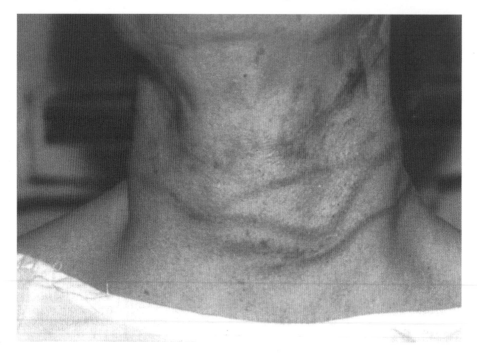

Strangler to kill his thirteen victims in the early 1960s was tied in a characteristic knot that identified each of the deaths as his handiwork.

The use of a ligature requires less pressure on the victim than is necessary in manual strangulation. As a result there is less obvious bruising around the neck, the cartilage of the larynx and windpipe may be intact, and there may be less muscular damage. Other hemorrhages may be revealed by blood in the brain tissues, for example, and there may also be damage to the neck muscles and thyroid cartilage.

Some victims found dead with a ligature around the neck are suicides. In such cases the

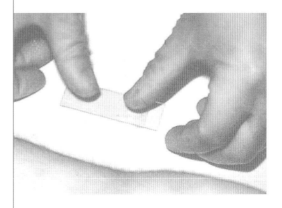

ABOVE A pathologist applies transparent adhesive tape to a ligature mark to lift any fibers onto paper for microscopic examination.

OPPOSITE The sensitive skin around the neck can reveal bruises from the strangler's fingers or abrasion from a strangling cord.

BELOW Murder equipment used by British serial killer Denis Nilson to torture and kill his victims.

ligature is usually deliberately tied with a double knot in order to maintain the pressure even as the victim loses consciousness. It may even be wound two or three times around the neck to make sure. However in suicide cases, the hyoid bone is usually found to be intact.

Hanging

The scene of a hanging usually betrays all too clearly what has happened, but still two main questions face forensic examiners. First, did the victim die from hanging, or was he or she already dead before the body was hanged? And second, if the victim died as a result of the hanging, was it murder or was it suicide?

Hanging is a special case of a ligature strangulation where the pressure around the neck is maintained by gravity acting on the victim's body. This causes the neck to be compressed, which closes off the vessels supplying blood to the brain and also the air passages, causing a loss of consciousness, and then death by asphyxia follows shortly after.

Other indications of the manner of death depend on how far the body has fallen, or the force with which the body fell, during the hanging. If the drop was only slight, there may

be relatively little damage to the neck muscles, although there is often thyroid damage, and the hyoid bone is usually broken. If the body has dropped a matter of feet, then the neck muscles may be ruptured and the spine dislocated from the shock of the noose suddenly tightening around the neck under the full weight of the body.

Hanging victims can die without actually being clear of the floor. Suicides who lack a strong enough overhead fitting have succeeded in hanging themselves from furniture or doorknobs. Falling from a crouching position can exert the necessary pressure to the neck, even though most of the body weight is still supported by the floor. Dying by this method

BELOW The mummified body of Tollund Man dating from 240–20 BC. This well preserved body found in Jutland, Denmark belonged to a man aged between 30 and 40, hanged with a braided leather noose in either a murder or a religious sacrifice.

usually takes longer than it does by conventional hanging, and forensic examiners usually find signs of gradual asphyxia in the victim. These include a swollen face with a purple tinge and many pinpoint hemorrhages around the eyes, as well as in the voice box and windpipe.

In the eighteenth-century in England, when hanging was a common penalty for even trivial crimes, the convict was tied up, the noose placed around the neck, then he or she was hoisted off the ground by the rope. If the noose was not pulled sufficiently tight, the unfortunate criminal could take a long time to die, and it became common for friends, relatives, or the executioner—if suitably bribed—to hasten death by hanging on to the criminal's feet, thereby increasing the pressure on the neck. Later, efforts were made to ensure a quicker death by using a tighter noose and a longer drop. The rope then tightened with a jerk, dislocating the neck and severing the spinal cord, leading to almost instantaneous death of the victim.

ABOVE Re-enactment of a murder by hanging at Blackfriars Bridge, London.

LEFT A public hanging at Tyburn in London, in the early 17th century.

Michel Eyraud

In the high summer of 1889, the small riverside community of Millery near Lyon in southern France was disturbed by a terrible smell. A council workman was sent to investigate, and found a rotting corpse, tied up in a canvas sack, among bushes by the riverbank. The remains were taken to the Lyon city morgue, a barge on the River Rhône that smelled strongly of the investigations conducted on board. There the local forensic pathologist, Dr. Paul Bernard, began his examination.

Though the identity of the body was a mystery, Dr. Bernard found the injuries to the neck showed that the victim had died from strangulation, possibly with a ligature. Evidence from the skull led him to suggest that the victim's age had been about thirty-five.

Police investigations turned up a trunk that smelled as strongly as the body and had almost certainly been used to transport it. The trunk's labels showed that it had been sent from Paris to Lyon just over two weeks before the discovery of the remains. Checks of the missing persons files in Paris revealed that a notorious womanizer called Toussaint-Augsent Gouffé had been reported missing on the day that the trunk had been dispatched to Lyon. Assumptions that the corpse was that of the missing Gouffé were initially confounded when the man's brother-in-law reported that Gouffé had chestnut-colored hair: the hair and beard of the corpse were both jet black.

LEFT Engraving showing a reconstruction of the Gouffé murder.

When Dr. Bernard soaked a hair sample in distilled water, however, the black dissolved to reveal a bright chestnut color. The corpse was then delivered to the foremost criminal pathologist in France and a pioneer of scientific detection, Dr. Alexandre Lacassagne, professor of forensic medicine at the University of Lyon. Dr. Lacassagne was convinced that death had been caused by manual strangulation. Examination of the bones also showed a defect in the right knee which would have produced a definite limp. After studying the victim's teeth, he amended Bernard's estimate of the victim's age to about fifty. Since Gouffé had been forty-nine and had walked with a noticeable limp, the identity of the corpse seemed certain, especially when samples of hair from the corpse were matched with hairs from Gouffé's own hairbrush.

A huge publicity campaign, aided by a replica of the trunk used to transport Gouffé's remains to Lyon, produced a pair of suspects: Michel Eyraud and his mistress Gabrielle Bompard, who had been seen buying a similar trunk in Paris. It later emerged that the pair had lured Gouffé to Bompard's apartment, where they intended to kill him before raiding his offices. They tried to hang him by winding Bompard's dressing-gown cord around his neck and then passing it over an overhead pulley, but the knot failed to hold. Eyraud was forced to strangle Gouffé with his bare hands, after which the couple ransacked his office but failed to find most of his money.

After sending the trunk with Gouffé's remains to Lyon, the pair fled to North America. When Eyraud suggested repeating the crime they parted company, and Bompard returned to France. Eyraud was caught almost two years later in Cuba, and finally extradited to France where the couple were tried for murder. Bompard was given a twenty-year sentence, and Eyraud was sent to the guillotine.

ABOVE Engraving showing the arrest of Michel Eyraud in Havana, Cuba.

LEFT A replica of the trunk used to transport the remains of Gouffé's body, which was first identified by its smell.

Drowning and Burning

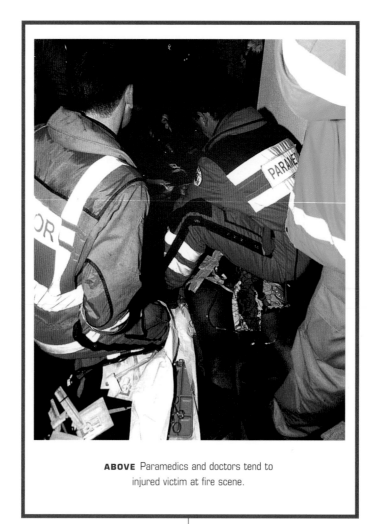

ABOVE Paramedics and doctors tend to
injured victim at fire scene.

Drowning and burning are two further
circumstances in which a victim may have
suffered an accident or murderous attack, or
have committed suicide. Deaths by drowning
or burning are usually brought about by tragic
accidents, though once again forensic experts
check carefully that the apparent circumstances
are indeed those in which the victim died, and
have not simply been used to obliterate evidence
of a more sinister death.

When a body is found dead in water in any
circumstances—including lying face down in a
puddle—forensic scientists must determine
whether the victim died of drowning or
hypothermia as a result of being in the water,
or whether he or she was already dead before
falling or being placed in the water.

From the medical point of view, drowning
has similarities to asphyxia or suffocation, in
that the victim dies because air cannot reach

the lungs, blocked in drowning by water, and the body is starved of oxygen. Signs indicating this lack of oxygen are revealed in the systems of genuine drowning victims, but the clarity of the evidence depends largely on how fiercely the victim fought to escape drowning. In a few cases of accidental drowning, a person falls into water while heavily intoxicated, so the struggle to survive is not as intense or as prolonged as that of a sober victim who is swept away in a swimming or boating accident and is fully aware of what is happening.

Evidence of drowning

A person drowns when water enters the lungs. This produces a fine frothy mixture of water, air, and mucus that appears at the mouth and nostrils. The weight of water in the lungs causes the body to swell and increase in weight so that it tends to float lower in the water than a live person would.

The body of a victim who has fallen into a swollen river or been swept away in an accident may provide additional indications of the circumstances. If he or she clutched at the banks or at foliage in an attempt to reach safety, soil, stones, twigs or leaves may still be held in the hands in the vice-like grip caused by muscular spasms in the final phases of drowning.

Injuries on the body are more difficult to interpret. The signs that normally indicate whether the injuries that caused death occurred before or after the body entered the water may be blurred by the effects of immersion, which can cause chemical changes to the blood, for example. If the water is fast-moving, as in river rapids or where waves break on rocks, the body may sustain severe injuries after death by drowning: the clarity of the evidence depends largely on the length of time the body remained in the water.

The autopsy provides more detailed evidence. After death by drowning, the lungs appear waterlogged, swollen, and soft to the touch, so that pressure on the surface of the lungs leaves

BELOW A bound body recovered from the water may not be a murder victim. Suicides often tie themselves up, and put weights in their clothes to ensure their attempts to take their own lives succeed.

a mark that is comparatively slow to fade. The frothy mixture of water, air, and mucus that appears in the nose and mouth of the victim is also present in the windpipe and lungs, and in many cases water is found in the throat and stomach. The stomach may also contain organisms from the water in which the body was found. In addition, most genuine cases of drowning show hemorrhages in the middle ear that are not present if, for example, the victim had died from heart failure or upon falling into the water.

There are apparent drowning cases where the victim does not actually die from drowning, but from the shock of suddenly being plunged into cold water. This condition is called "reflex cardiac arrest," and the victim dies from a heart attack rather than from the oxygen starvation caused by the interruption of the body's air supply. In these cases, the normal signs of drowning will not be found on the body. Sometimes victims who were deeply intoxicated when they fell into the water may die from this condition. In other cases, they can drown in a puddle only inches deep because the mouth and nostrils were under water, and anoxia resulted before they realized what was happening.

Examining the clues

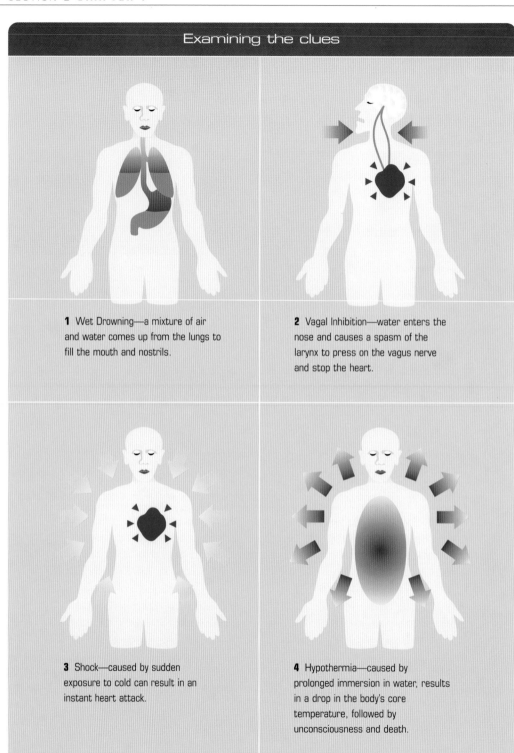

1 Wet Drowning—a mixture of air and water comes up from the lungs to fill the mouth and nostrils.

2 Vagal Inhibition—water enters the nose and causes a spasm of the larynx to press on the vagus nerve and stop the heart.

3 Shock—caused by sudden exposure to cold can result in an instant heart attack.

4 Hypothermia—caused by prolonged immersion in water, results in a drop in the body's core temperature, followed by unconsciousness and death.

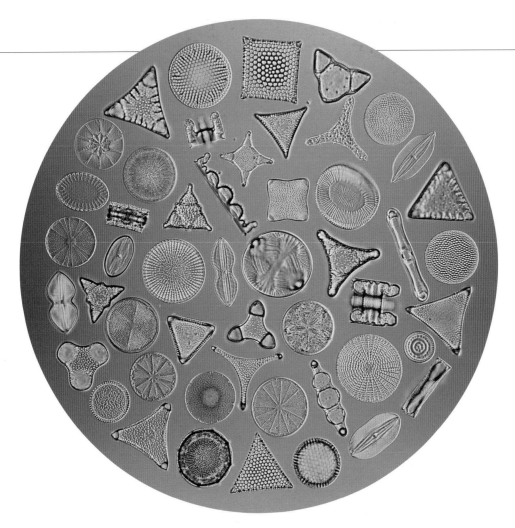

Time of drowning

The process of decay in water is different than that which occurs in bodies buried, or left exposed on land. First of all, in water the cooling process after death occurs twice as quickly, and in cases where a victim suffered death from hypothermia rather than by drowning, the core temperature of the body may already be appreciably lower than normal when the process of post-mortem cooling begins to set in.

Post-mortem lividity is less obvious with a corpse immersed in water: here the skin appears unnaturally white, with a "goose-flesh" effect from when the body's hair follicles became erect, a reflex intended to retain body heat as long as possible. Rigor mortis can take longer to develop and longer to disappear because the temperature of the water slows

ABOVE Diatoms, microscopic algae-like creatures found in the lungs, stomach, bloodstream, and bone marrow of drowning victims.

down the chemical processes that trigger these post-mortem changes. A body may be in water for up to four full days before all traces of rigor disappear.

After a week or more in the water, chemical changes within the body cause the abdomen to fill with gas. This increases the buoyancy of the body so that it floats on the surface of the water. As a result, many drowning victims not retrieved earlier tend to be found at this stage. The conversion of body fats into a hard residue, which normally takes place after around four to six months on land, may take much longer in water, particularly if the temperature is low.

Place of drowning

Blood tests can indicate whether a victim died by drowning in fresh or in saltwater, provided tests are carried out soon enough after death. Fresh water, found in rivers, ponds, and most lakes as well as canals and other inland waterways, is able to pass through the tiny blood vessels in the lungs and find its way into the heart and the rest of the circulatory system, where it has the effect of diluting the blood and reducing its chlorine content.

The salt in sea water, on the other hand, absorbs water from the blood, thereby increasing the proportion of chlorine present instead of diluting it. This clearly defined difference can help investigators faced with a body found where a river enters tidal water: the chemical changes that occurred when the victim drowned can indicate where and when the incident took place.

Another accurate pointer to the place of drowning involves analyzing body organs for the presence of tiny organisms called diatoms (see p. 103). These are present in all water sources that contain normal biosystems. A victim of drowning inhales these organisms along with the water that causes the drowning, and they are absorbed into the internal organs. When the autopsy is carried out, the presence of diatoms can be verified by dissolving sections of the internal organs in strong acids, which then reveal the silica shells of the diatoms if they are present. The shells can then be identified by close inspection under a microscope.

The presence of diatoms in a waterborne body gives two useful clues. First, it indicates that the victim was almost certainly alive when he or she entered the water. Second, there are many different species of these organisms and they are identifiable by the shape and size of their skeletons, so the species or combination of species found in the victim's body may help to show the approximate area where the original drowning took place.

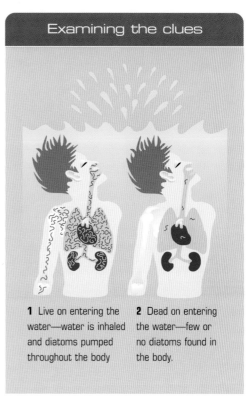

Examining the clues

1 Live on entering the water—water is inhaled and diatoms pumped throughout the body

2 Dead on entering the water—few or no diatoms found in the body.

TOP A victim of Wayne Williams (see pages 60-1) lies face down in a boat after being pulled from the Chattahoochee river.

OPPOSITE Retrieving a body to find the cause and time of death.

Burning victims

As with drowning, cases of burning are more often than not the result of accidents rather than of homicide, though here too investigators must bear in mind that the body may have been deliberately burned in an attempt to disguise some other cause of death. This involves checking the body to determine which of the injuries were caused by burning, whether or not those injuries were inflicted before or after death, and which factors actually caused death.

There are six degrees of burn injuries, classified in ascending order of severity according to a scheme first set out by French surgeon Baron Guillaume Dupuytren almost two centuries ago. First-degree burns cause the skin to become inflamed and swollen and scales of the skin surface to be shed. Second-degree burns show blistering, third- and fourth-degree burns show partial or entire destruction of the victim's skin, and fifth-degree burns destroy the muscles. Sixth-degree burns, the most severe, also show bone destruction. Burn injuries are also classified in terms of the percentage of body area affected.

Many victims found in burned-out structures die from smoke suffocation or carbon monoxide poisoning, which happen

LEFT A fire at the entrance of the Happyland nightclub in New York's Bronx caused 87 deaths.

OPPOSITE ABOVE London's King's Cross disaster, in 1987, where smoke and fire poured through a crowded subway station.

quickly, rather than from the burns themselves. In such cases the autopsy shows signs of oxygen starvation. This may be caused by smoke inhalation, a possibility that can be confirmed by the presence of soot particles in the windpipe. Blood tests can also show the presence of carbon monoxide at a level high enough to cause death, while the presence of any carbon monoxide or soot within the victim's body confirms he or she was still alive when the fire started. If none of these signs are found, then the victim must have been dead before the blaze took hold.

Examination of the victim's burns can give an indication of the sequence of events. In general, burns suffered while the victim was still alive have a higher proportion of white cells in the blood count, because the body's natural defenses mobilized at the time in an effort to contain the damage. Fluid from the blisters at the site of the burns can also be tested for proteins: their presence indicates that the victim was alive when they formed.

Some severe burns—even those sustained after death—can cause the body tissues to rupture in a manner very similar to that caused by a battering from fists or blunt instruments. But careful analysis shows whether or not there has been underlying bleeding as a result of the wounds. If the splitting of the tissues was caused by heat, the blood will already have coagulated and there will be no signs of bleeding, as there would be in injuries caused by battering.

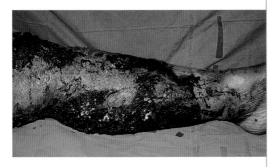

ABOVE Severe leg burns caused by the hot fat from a deep frier pan.

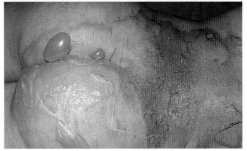

ABOVE Blistering and skin ruptures on the back of a fire accident victim.

Robert Maxwell

ABOVE Maxwell's yacht, the *Lady Ghislaine*.

BELOW Robert Maxwell shortly before his death in 1991.

In the fall of 1991, British publisher and newspaper tycoon Robert Maxwell was cruising in his luxury yacht, the *Lady Ghislaine*. One morning the crew was shocked to find he was no longer on board. He had last been seen on deck the evening before. A search was made and his dead body was eventually found in the sea off the Canary Islands in the northeast Atlantic Ocean. The subsequent enquiry came under the jurisdiction of the Spanish authorities, because the Canary Islands group is Spanish territory.

At the time, press speculation centered on Maxwell's known links with Israel and his rumored involvement with Mossad, the Israeli intelligence service, and there was a suggestion that his connections may have made him the target of a sophisticated professional assassination. Had that been the case, Maxwell would almost certainly have been dead before he entered the water, since otherwise the alarm might have been raised and Maxwell could have been rescued.

Spanish experts carried out an autopsy and found that diatoms were present in Maxwell's blood and body tissues, showing clearly that he had died after he entered the water. There was no evidence of other injuries to suggest that a murder attempt had taken place, but one curious feature of the body was the fact that the lungs were not full of water. This

could have been due to a condition known as "dry drowning," where the shock of falling into the water causes a spasm of the larynx. This triggers a body reflex which is similar to the reaction of the system to a sudden and severe increase in blood pressure: the heart stops, bringing about death in seconds. The only question the enquiry could not answer was whether Maxwell had entered the water accidentally or deliberately, since rumors of the shakiness of his business empire could have motivated him to make a suicide attempt.

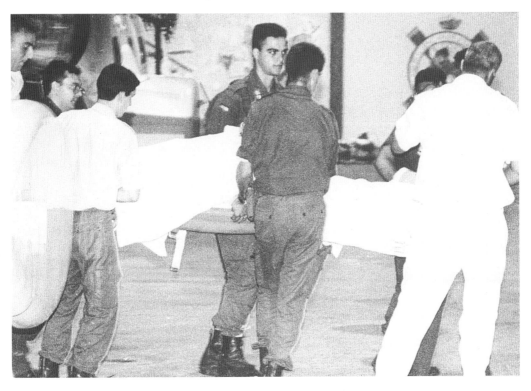

The Smoking Gun

ABOVE This 19th century engraving of French and Austrian soldiers at Edelsberg Bridge near Vienna in 1809 shows how the short range of smooth-bore muskets led to fighting at very close quarters.

Ever since smooth-bore pistols and muskets were replaced by mass-produced rifled weapons (in the late eighteenth century, around the time of the War of Independence), each spent bullet has had an individual tale to tell. Thanks to the process of rifling, cutting internal helical grooves similar to a screw thread in the barrel of a firearm, the fired bullet spins as it emerges from the barrel. This prevents the projectile from tumbling in flight and greatly increases its accuracy, making rifled weapons essential for hunters and soldiers alike.

RIGHT Bullets and spent cartridges can provide vital evidence.

From the viewpoint of forensic scientists, the main benefit of rifling is not that it makes a bullet fly more predictably to its target, but the fact that it imparts an individual identity to every single gun. When bullets are fired through the barrel, the rifling grooves create marks on the bullet's surface in a pattern unique to that weapon, and a similar pattern of marks appears on any bullet fired from that weapon, because the material of which bullets are made is softer than that of gun barrels.

When bullets were introduced that were encapsulated with the explosive charge in a single cased cartridge, more clues became available to investigators. As a charge explodes within the barrel it expands in both directions, driving the bullet forward and the cartridge case backward with considerable force against the breech of the weapon. The case, ejected as the shot is fired, carries imprint details of imperfections in the face of the breech and of parts of the gun mechanism such as the firing pin. These patterns once again vary from

weapon to weapon, but are virtually identical on any cartridge case used in a particular firearm.

ABOVE Weapons used in crime include revolvers and automatics, rifles and sawed-off shotguns.

BELOW High-speed photo of a .30 revolver bullet cutting through a playing card from edge to edge.

Classes of weapon

In mass-produced guns, particular makes and models of weapon are given the same standardized characteristics, including the barrel's internal diameter or caliber, the number of grooves in its rifling, and the direction in which the grooves spiral from breech to muzzle. This is very useful to forensic examiners and helps them to deduce the make and class of the weapon from any bullets found at the scene of a crime or in the body of a gunshot victim.

For example, Colt and Browning revolvers both have six grooves in the rifling, but those in the Colt turn anti-clockwise, whereas those in the Browning turn clockwise. Webley revolvers also have a clockwise spiral but have seven rifling grooves, while Smith and Wesson weapons have a clockwise spiral and only five grooves. Other variations between one make of weapon and another lie in the relative width of the rifling grooves and the "lands," the sections of barrel that are left between successive grooves.

Firearm "fingerprints"

While the design differences between different classes, makes and models of weapon can help identify which kind was used at a specific

ABOVE The classic Colt .45—the double-action Army revolver.

crime, the evidence needed for a positive identification of an individual weapon must be much more precise. The internal surfaces of an individual barrel carry fine lines or striations on both the grooves and the lands. These are

BELOW A French forensic laboratory analyzing the interior of a gun barrel.

ABOVE The compact Smith & Wesson .38 revolver.

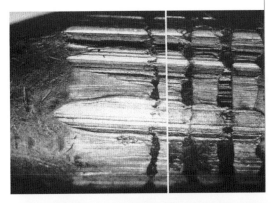

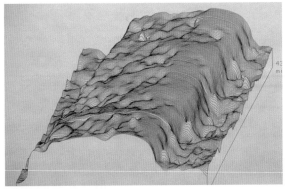

caused by surface defects on the cutting tool used to make the barrel, or by chips of steel scratched across the barrel's internal surfaces by the action of the cutter.

Unless the barrel is cut open for analysis, however, these striations normally remain unseen and cannot be recorded and measured. Nevertheless, the striations present in the barrel of each individual gun produce a characteristic set of marks on any bullet fired from that barrel. By firing a test bullet from a suspect weapon, then lining it up in a comparison microscope alongside a bullet from the crime scene, a positive match of these individual markings can be made with a greater degree of accuracy.

The New York Bureau of Forensic Ballistics was founded in 1923 by Charles Waite and Philip Gravelle. Waite was a deputy district attorney who had been appalled to see an innocent man almost executed six years previously because of worthless testimony regarding the identification of the murder weapon. Gravelle was the microscopist who invented the comparison microscope, a piece of equipment now indispensable to ballistics investigations (see Chapter One).

Waite died in 1926, but by then Calvin Goddard, a U.S. Army medical doctor and firearms expert, had joined the team. Goddard used Waite's collection of information on the standard calibers and rifling features of

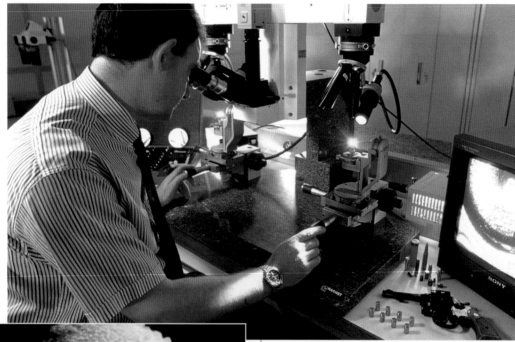

ABOVE Using a comparison microscope.

LEFT Scanning electron microscope image of particles of firing residue.

different makes and models of guns to great advantage. He also developed forensic ballistic techniques by working with the comparison microscope and a device called a helixometer, a hollow probe fitted with a light source and a magnifying lens that allows examination of the marks on the inside of a gun barrel.

The comparison microscope used for ballistics examinations has two cylindrical bullet-holders side by side beneath the examining lens system. Each of the holders can be rotated independently so that similar

parts of the surface of the two bullets can be lined up to find a matching pattern. They can then be rotated simultaneously to compare other points of resemblance.

Experts cannot always establish a match complete in all respects. Sometimes particles of grit or rust within the barrel alter some of the markings impressed on bullets fired at different times. If a series of bullets has been fired between the firing of the suspect bullet and the test bullet, some internal wear of the barrel will have taken place in the intervening period. Similarly, if the bullet found at the crime scene is distorted, having passed through the victim's body or other obstructions, establishing a match is not straightforward. With expert knowledge and experience, however, it is usually possible.

Shotguns

The shotgun is an important exception as far as rifling is concerned. Instead of firing a single bullet, the explosion of the charge in the cartridge discharges a spray of small lead pellets which diverge as they fly through the air. Shotguns may be single- or double-barreled; in the latter the two barrels are arranged either side by side or one on top of the other. Each barrel usually needs to be reloaded once the cartridge has been fired. This is done by "breaking" the gun, folding the barrels downward to open the breeches and allow the discharged cartridges to be ejected and new ones to be fitted. The gun is then "cocked" by closing the breeches. Single-barreled shotguns are reloaded in exactly the same way.

Other types of shotgun, known as "pump-action" guns, carry several cartridges in an internal magazine, so the user can reload by pushing a slider backward and forward. Shotguns used for hunting have long barrels to minimize the spread of the pellets as far as possible, thus extending the weapon's lethal range. Shotguns are sometimes used by criminals at short range, however, a foot or more having been sawed off the barrels' length makes the guns easier to hide. At almost point-blank range, where the shotgun is most dangerous to a human target, the spread of the pellets is negligible.

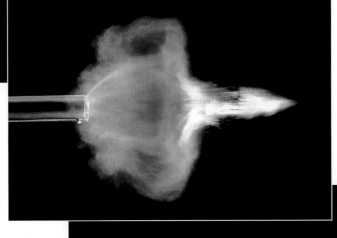

ABOVE High speed photograph of a charge of pellets leaving the muzzle of a 12-bore shotgun, taken 2.8 milliseconds after detonation.

ABOVE RIGHT Four milliseconds after the cartridge detonates, a puff of smoke and gunpowder residues leave the barrel in the wake of the shot.

RIGHT The plastic wad separating from the shot after 5.7 milliseconds.

RIGHT After 7 milliseconds, particles of the wad that seals the front end of the cartridge falls away, and the charge of pellets begins to spread out.

Gunshot wounds

The appearance of a gunshot wound depends on the range at which the weapon was fired. Establishing the range is important in helping forensic investigators to determine exactly what happened. A case of apparent suicide would be immediately suspicious if the evidence showed that the gun had been fired from farther than arm's length from the victim's body. Equally, a claim of self-defense may be easier to prove if the evidence shows that the gun was shot at close range, when discharging the weapon might have been the user's last line of defense.

In cases where victim and assailant are at close quarters, and particularly where a struggle is taking place, the gun may be fired with the muzzle pressing against the victim's body. In such cases, the hot gases and soot particles produced by the discharge of the cartridge are driven into the skin and cause burning at the edges of the wound. If the wound was made through clothing, then the fibers around the hole in the cloth made by the bullet may be scorched or melted by the heat of the discharge, and the material may show a star-shaped tear pattern around the bullet hole.

If the gun is held more loosely against the body of the victim, there may be room for the

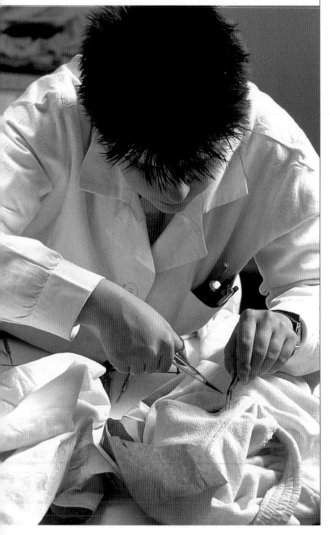

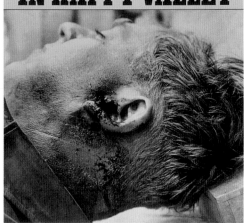

ABOVE Photo of the body of Josslyn Hay, 22nd Earl of Erroll, found dead from a gunshot wound to the head, in the "Happy Valley" scandal in Kenya in 1941.

LEFT Forensic examiner checking the clothing around a bullet hole for signs of the range at which the weapon was fired.

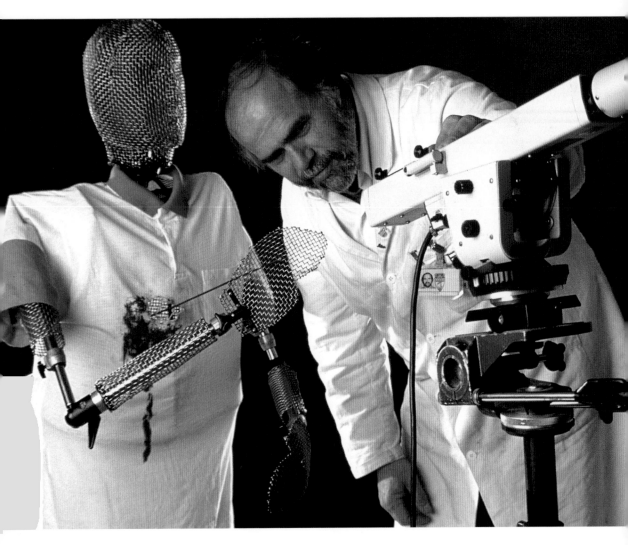

hot gases to escape through the gap between muzzle and victim. The gases, carrying particles of soot with them, then leave a wider ring of discolored skin around the entry wound. If the gun is pointing straight at the victim, the ring will be circular, but if it is pointed at an angle, the ring will be distorted into an oval mark, its longest axis lying along the angle at which the gun barrel was held.

If the weapon is fired from a slightly longer range, then particles of unburned and partly-burned powder are driven into the skin, causing a pattern called "tattooing." If the victim was alive when the wound was inflicted, the tattooing is usually orange or brown in color, but if the wound was inflicted when the victim was already dead, then the color is a

more subdued gray-yellow. If the wound is inflicted through the victim's clothing, the powder residues leave a clearly visible pattern, the spread of which is an indication of the range at which the shot was fired.

To make the most accurate estimation of the range, a ballistics examiner usually fires the suspect weapon from varying distances into cloth or fabric that is as similar to the victim's clothing as possible. The range that leaves the pattern most closely resembling that on the victim's clothing, given identical ammunition, is then the most likely range at which the shot was fired.

Entry and exit wounds

Examiners can expect to find patterns of soot around a bullet wound if it was made from a range of between twelve and eighteen inches. Scattered specks of unburned and partially-burned powder grains can be found if the shot was fired at a range of up to twenty-five inches, and scattered grains are occasionally found where the range was up to thirty-six inches. Beyond that distance, the only extraneous marking found around a bullet entry wound is a dark ring called "bullet wipe." The mark, made up of lead, carbon, oil and dirt, is brushed from the surface of the bullet as it enters the body.

In most cases the gunshot wound shows a circular or oval entry hole, drilled through the tissues by the shape of the bullet. By the time the bullet leaves the victim's body, it may have been distorted by impact with bone, or caused to tumble on its way through. Both these circumstances tend to produce exit wounds larger and more irregularly shaped than entry wounds, and there is no abrasion of the skin around the cavity.

Shotgun wounds, being caused by a spray of small particles, are entirely different. The degree of spread of the particles forms a measure of the range at which the gun was fired. At very short ranges, the shot has hardly any chance to spread and the whole charge tears a deep and concentrated wound through layers of the victim's body, leaving localized scorching and tattooing.

When the gun is fired more than three feet away from the victim's body, the pattern of holes caused by the pellets penetrating the skin begins to spread. At ranges of more than four feet the severity of the wound begins to reduce as the pattern of pellet-holes widens still further, leaving no sign of powder marking. However, the spread depends on the design of the weapon and the amount of "choke" or constriction of the barrel present. The choke is designed to extend the weapon's range by reducing the spread of the shot on leaving the muzzle. Once again the only reliable way for a forensic examiner to determine the range of the shot is to fire a series of test shots with the gun used in a particular incident to find the range at which the spread most closely resembles the signs found on the victim.

ABOVE Taking a swab from a suspect's hand to test for microscopic particles of gunpowder, and the presence of chemicals like cordite, widely used in cartridges as a propellant.

OPPOSITE PAGE The bodyguard of the speaker of the Egyptian Parliament, Rifaat al-Mahgoub, killed by a spray of automatic fire in a successful assassination attempt.

RIGHT Head X-ray of a murder victim shows groups of shotgun pellets across the face, and at the left-hand end of the jaw.

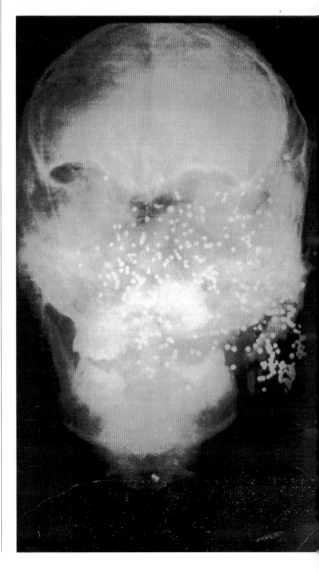

Other types of weapon

Most firearms other than shotguns are categorized as either handguns or rifles. Handguns can be revolvers or pistols. Revolvers have a series of cartridges loaded into a cylindrical magazine which moves around at the discharge of each shot to bring the next round into the breech. They can be "single-action," where the user has to pull back the hammer to rotate the magazine and cock the firing mechanism, or "double-action," where this is achieved automatically by pressing hard on the trigger. Automatic pistols, on the other hand, usually have a series of rounds held in a vertical magazine inside the handle of the weapon. All the user has to do to fire the weapon is pull the trigger: the ejection of the spent cartridge, the loading of the next round into the breech and the cocking of the weapon are all carried out by the gun's own internal mechanism.

ABOVE Massed ranks of seized handguns in a court office.

LEFT A salesman demonstrates a Smith & Wesson .357 Magnum pistol in Florida, 1987.

Rifles can be classified as target, sporting or military, and their actions vary in a similar way to those of handguns. Many rifles carry a series of rounds in an internal magazine, but most use a bolt action to reload. When the bolt is pulled back, the spent cartridge is ejected; when it is pushed forward and turned, it pushes a new round into the breech and cocks the firing mechanism. Other rifles, particularly those designed for military use, eject the used round and load a new one by automatic action, so again all the user has to do is pull the trigger.

Not all weapons use explosively-propelled bullets. Poachers and hunters have traditionally used quieter air-operated weapons to shoot game. Commercially-made airguns and air pistols are hardly the most powerful weapons, though they can produce a serious wound at short range. Occasionally, however, investigators have had to deal with more powerful homemade weapons charged with compressed air and designed to fire larger, more deadly projectiles.

Another type of ballistic weapon, which has little in common with firearms, is the powerful crossbow used by archers in the Middle Ages. A handful of criminals in the United Kingdom and at least one in Canada have used crossbows, which are operated by tightening a short and exceedingly powerful bow with a pair of cranked handles. When the bow is fired, it releases a short steel bolt with lethal force and almost silent operation. Alternatively the classic English long bow, beloved of medieval outlaw Robin Hood, can fire an arrow with sufficient force to penetrate a suit of armor, and a skilled archer can fire a third arrow while the first and second are still in flight.

ABOVE The battle of Agincourt in 1415, where ranks of humbly-born English long bowmen slaughtered the flower of French chivalry with rapid volleys of arrows, deadly accurate and lethal through full armor.

LEFT Author and keen hunter Ernest Hemingway nets two pheasants. On July 2, 1961, depressed over his work, he committed suicide with a shotgun at his home in Ketchum, Idaho.

Bullets and cartridges

For more than one hundred and fifty years, the design of cartridges for both handguns and rifles has followed the same general pattern. A cylindrical cartridge case, usually made of brass, holds the main propellant charge used to fire the bullet. The front end of the cartridge is sealed by the bullet, and at the back a small cap contains a charge of primer. When the gun is fired, the firing pin strikes the cap and detonates the primer, which then sets off the main charge and fires the bullet straight down the barrel.

A ballistics expert can usually link the shape and design of the cartridge to a particular type and model of gun. Some cartridges have the primer cap in the center and others have the primer arranged around the rim of the cartridge case; there are also differences in the bullets used in the cartridges, and all this information can help the expert to identify the ammunition used in a given incident.

Most pistols and rifles used for sport or target-shoot purposes use lead bullets. These may be round-nosed, sharp-nosed, cylindrical or hollow-pointed so that they expand on

ABOVE Analyzing the marks left by the impact of the firing pin on the end of the cartridge case, for comparison.

RIGHT An instrument which can measure the pattern of surface roughness around a bullet, for identification.

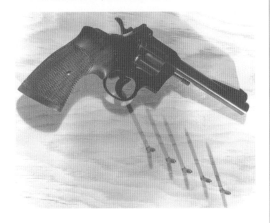

ABOVE Colt revolver and bullets.

impact. They are essentially "soft" bullets and would be unsuitable for high-velocity weapons such as military rifles and automatic pistols. Such weapons use bullets with a lead or steel core that is wholly or partially enclosed in a jacket made of aluminum or alloys of copper with zinc or nickel. Specialized armor-piercing, tracer or incendiary bullets are also used in more sophisticated military weapons.

Shotgun cartridges are larger versions of rifle and pistol cartridges and comprise a charge, a case and a primer cap. Instead of a bullet, the front end of the cartridge is sealed by a wad, a disk of compressed cardboard, and a plastic body filled with small shotgun pellets. Crimped cardboard holds the pellets in place. Some shotgun cartridges, intended for shooting at large animals such as deer or bears, are fitted with solid, large-caliber bullets.

Sacco and Vanzetti

ABOVE Bullets recovered from the body of Allesandro Berardelli, together with cartridges found at the scene—the third bullet from the left, deformed by impact, inflicted the fatal wound.

ABOVE Calvin Goddard inspecting a gun barrel with a helixometer.

On the afternoon of April 15, 1920, two security guards were delivering a shoe-company payroll of more than $15,000 in the small Massachusetts town of South Braintree. Two men suddenly appeared and opened fire, killing both security guards. They seized the cash and loaded it into a getaway car before driving off at high speed. Horrified eye-witnesses reported that the men were of "Italian" appearance, and one had a prominent drooping mustache. Police searching the scene discovered a range of spent cartridges that were later identified as having been manufactured by three different munitions companies: Peters, Remington and Winchester.

The getaway car was found abandoned in woodland, and a search revealed links to an earlier robbery that implicated an Italian criminal named Boda. When police raided his house they found he had fled, leaving behind the heavily mustached Bartolomeo Vanzetti, aged thirty-two, and Nicola Sacco, aged twenty-nine. Both men were carrying loaded pistols. Sacco's was of the same caliber as one of the guns used to murder the guards, and in his pockets were cartridges made by Peters, Remington and Winchester. Both men were arrested and charged with murder.

It emerged that the men belonged to an anarchist movement that openly advocated violence to settle society's injustices, and their trial sharply polarized opinion. The prosecution insisted the men were guilty, while defense attorneys insisted that they were being persecuted for their beliefs. As far as the ballistics evidence was concerned, each side produced experts whose testimonies contradicted the others'.

The outcome of the trial ultimately depended on whether or not the bullet that had killed one of the guards, Alessandro Berardelli, had been fired from Sacco's .32 pistol. The ballistics experts found that the bullet used was no longer in production, indeed it was so outdated that they could find no similar ammunition to use in firing test rounds—apart from the unused cartridges found in Sacco's pockets. After tests, the two bullets were compared and the match was close enough to secure a guilty verdict. The defendants were sentenced to death.

The verdict was overturned, however, after a self-styled expert named Alexander Hamilton appeared and denounced the ballistics evidence as false. Hamilton's evidence had succeeded in misleading a jury in a murder trial six years earlier, even though it had been scientifically worthless. At that trial Charles Waite, who went on to found the Bureau of Forensic Ballistics with his partner Philip Gravelle, had shown that Hamilton's assertion that a particular gun had been used as a murder weapon had almost convicted an innocent man. For the time being, however, Hamilton caused sufficient doubt to raise a motion for a retrial.

At the retrial, Hamilton brought two new Colt revolvers into court and dismantled them, together with Sacco's gun. When he was caught trying to fit one of the new barrels onto the alleged murder weapon, the retrial was cancelled. By June 1927, Calvin Goddard of the Bureau of Forensic Ballistics in New York was able to show that a test bullet fired from Sacco's revolver matched one of the murder bullets perfectly. He used a comparison microscope and a helixometer and produced evidence clear enough to convince even the defense experts, so Sacco and Vanzetti went to the electric chair on August 23, 1927.

Nevertheless, the legend grew that Sacco and Vanzetti had been put to death for a crime they had not committed, and in spite of the fact that a team of forensic experts re-confirmed in 1961 that Sacco's gun was the murder weapon, the governor of Massachusetts in 1977 issued a special proclamation establishing the men's innocence, half a century after their execution. Yet another investigation in 1983 reaffirmed the truth of the ballistics evidence. Nevertheless, to this day the case remains highly controversial.

RIGHT Vanzetti and Sacco (center and right) being led to court in handcuffs.

BACKGROUND One of the demonstrations organized in support of Sacco and Vanzetti.

Georgi Markov

ABOVE Bulgarian dissident Georgi Markov was the second to be attacked by agents of the Bulgarian government.

Some twenty years before the collapse of the communist regimes of Eastern Europe during the 1990s, Georgi Markov was a Bulgarian dissident working for the BBC World Service in London, broadcasting to his former homeland. On the afternoon of September 7, 1978, he was waiting for a bus on Waterloo Bridge when he felt a sharp stabbing pain in his right thigh. He turned to see a man carrying a furled umbrella; the man mumbled an apology in a thick accent and hurried off to hail a cab.

Once home, Markov inspected the wound. It was a small red puncture mark at the back of his leg. By the following morning he was vomiting and running a high temperature, and was taken to hospital where the wound, now inflamed, was X-rayed. Nothing suspicious showed up on the films, but his temperature and blood-pressure were now dropping and his pulse racing. His white-cell count soared to three times the normal level and doctors suspected blood poisoning. He was treated with antibiotics but became delirious and subject to violent fits. He eventually died four days after the mysterious wound had been inflicted.

An autopsy was carried out and the section of tissue that contained the puncture wound was sent to the Porton Down chemical warfare research laboratories. There experts found, buried beneath the skin, a spherical pellet approximately the size of a pinhead with two tiny holes drilled in it. No trace could be found of any poison that might have caused Markov's illness and death, and the pellet was sent to the Metropolitan Police forensic laboratory where it was examined under a scanning electron microscope.

The pellet proved to be made of an alloy of platinum and iridium that was exceedingly hard and immune to corrosion—and virtually invisible on an X-ray plate. The holes in the pellet were large enough to hold a minute trace of poison, but their contents had dissipated. It was thought that the tiny pellet had been fired by some form of gas-operated gun hidden in the furled umbrella in a bid to assassinate Georgi Markov.

Identifying the poison became a process of elimination. Considering the minute size of the dose and its catastrophic effects, it was decided that the pellet must have been charged

BACKGROUND The specialized pellet gun concealed in the furled umbrella and used to murder Markov.

with ricin (see Chapter Four), a potential chemical warfare agent five hundred times more lethal than cyanide. The theory was tested by injecting a pig with a quantity of ricin similar to that which could have been contained in the pellet. The animal died within twenty-four hours, and its organs showed damage similar to that found at Markov's autopsy.

Though the Bulgarians denied any responsibility for the murder, another expatriate Bulgarian named Vladimir Kostov had suffered a similar attack in Paris a year earlier, but had recovered because the pellet had been fired into his back, well away from the main blood vessels. When a surgeon examined him, an identical pellet was found buried beneath his skin.

Following a change of regime in Bulgaria in 1991, the new government admitted that assassination attempts had been made on a number of former citizens living in the West, including Markov and Kostov.

TOP Scanning electron microscope used to examine the fatal pellet.

ABOVE Photomicrograph of the fatal pellet recovered from Markov's body.

RIGHT London's Waterloo Bridge, where the fatal blow was delivered.

The USS *Iowa*

The U.S. Navy is the only service in the world to maintain battleships as part of its active fleet since the end of World War Two. The Iowa class have a main armament of nine sixteen-inch guns mounted in three triple turrets. Each gun can fire a shell weighing some 2700 pounds with a range of up to twenty-four miles. To provide the colossal energy needed to achieve this, the guns are loaded with between five and seven bags of nitro-cellulose explosive, each bag weighing 93.4 pounds, in addition to the heavy shells.

During a firing drill on the battleship USS *Iowa* on April 19, 1989, five bags of the explosive being loaded into the center gun of number two turret exploded without warning, killing forty-seven seamen, including the entire crew of the armored turret. A Navy investigation found that the explosion had been caused by sabotage on the part of the petty officer in charge of the gun turret, in an attempt to commit suicide and claim the life of a former friend working at the bottom level of the turret. Both men died in the explosion, but their families strongly criticized the Navy's findings.

The Senate Armed Services Committee decided to commission explosives experts at Sandia National Laboratories to carry out a full technical investigation. When they checked the drill used to load the gun, they found that once the shell was placed in the barrel, the bags of explosives were pushed slowly up the barrel by a power-operated rammer until they were close to, but not in contact with, the shell. On the day of the exercise, the left gun was loaded in forty-four seconds and the right gun in sixty-one seconds. A recording of intercom messages showed that the sailor controlling the rammer of the center gun had reported a problem: eighty-three seconds later, the charges exploded.

The naval investigators claimed that analysis of debris in the gun-barrel showed traces of steel wool, brake fluid and calcium hypochlorite. They insisted that this had been

RIGHT Gun turrets of the USS *Iowa*—number two turret is in the background with its guns trained out to the side.

deliberately placed in the barrel as an incendiary device and had set off the charges when the pressure of the rammer was applied. The Sandia experts analyzed the traces and found they were made up of steel fibers, calcium and chlorine. But these elements were also found in the other gun turrets of the USS *Iowa*, as well as in those of her sister ships USS *Wisconsin* and USS *New Jersey*. Traces of these elements were found in lubricants and cleaning fluids used in the gun turrets, and in some cases were also found in sea water.

If the Navy's theory that there had been a deliberate attempt at sabotage and suicide was mistaken, what had really caused the explosion? Examiners found that the rammer on the center gun was pushing the explosive bags two feet farther up the barrel than it should have done, and other evidence suggested that the sailor controlling the rammer had been inexperienced and had operated the rammer much too quickly. Both these factors may have led to the explosives being slammed against the bulk of the shell with some force, but tests showed that such action did not detonate them. However it was found that extra sticks of explosive had been arranged in a loose layer at the top of each bag to make up the weight, and this would have imposed the additional stress necessary to cause the explosion.

When tests were carried out by dropping a steel weight representing the rammer onto bags of explosive containing a loose top layer, the bags exploded. As a result the Navy was able to change the loading procedure and ensure that a similar accident could not happen. Had the explosion been ascribed to sabotage, more sailors might have died in similar circumstances.

RIGHT Bodies of the gun turret crew at Dover AFB, Delaware.

Fire and Explosives

ABOVE Remains of a house totally wrecked by a gas explosion.

The terrible power of fire and explosives to obliterate evidence is harnessed by criminals both to achieve their aims directly and to disguise crimes committed by other means. Buildings and property are deliberately destroyed for insurance fraud; letter bombs and remote-control devices eliminate specific targets; and evidence of violence and theft are burned in the hope that all possible links with the perpetrator will be destroyed. Nevertheless, as the techniques available to forensic examiners become increasingly sophisticated, this potential avenue of escape for the criminal becomes ever more remote.

Human bodies prove extraordinarily resistant to complete destruction by fire and explosives: the tiniest scraps of evidence can now provide viable leads for investigators. When homemade bombs have been constructed from chemicals, or even when commercial explosives have been used, sufficient residues remain at the scene to help identify, and in some cases locate, the perpetrators.

Sometimes these residues are well hidden, having soaked into what remains of the furnishings where the explosion took place. But investigators can produce a solution of the residues by removing all potentially absorbent

ABOVE Smoke patterns on the outside of a burned-out house.

RIGHT Fire in an apartment block.

BELOW Evidence from a fire, bagged and ready for examination.

materials from the crime scene and treating them in acetone. Any residues can then be tested by chromatography to give an accurate blueprint of the explosive materials present. A similar technique can be used at scenes of suspicious fires, to discover whether any highly flammable materials were used to help start or maintain the blaze.

Fires, like explosions, need a source of energy to trigger them. Materials burn only when enough heat is applied to raise them to their ignition temperature. The ignition temperature of kerosene, for example, is approximately 445° F, that of benzene is 1045° F.

In other more complex materials, such as wood or coal, sufficient heat must be applied to cause the chemical breakdown of the material and the release of gases, which then ignite and start the material burning.

Fires do not normally start spontaneously: even a gas leak needs a stray spark to set it off. But some materials generate their own sources of heat and can spontaneously combust. Coal is one example: temperatures at the center of a large stack can reach levels high enough to ignite it. Similarly, hay stacked in badly ventilated storehouses can reach high temperatures because of the heat produced by bacterial activity, and can eventually burst into flames without warning. But most fires, whether accidental or deliberate, leave some clue as to the heat source that started it, whether it was a lit match or a bolt of lightning.

Explosions are even less likely to occur unless a specific combination of ingredients has been brought together to cause a rapid chemical reaction. Close inspection of the aftermath almost always reveals traces of those ingredients.

Fires burn at different temperatures depending on their fuel. As a result, they burn with differing colors of flame and smoke. Wood and cloth fires, for example, burn with reddish-yellow flames and gray-brown smoke. Gasoline and kerosene fires burn with yellow-white flames and black smoke, and cooking oil burns with yellow flames and brown smoke.

Accident—or arson?

In any case of death apparently resulting from fire, a crucial part of the forensic examination is directed at determining the cause of the fire. If a victim's body has been burned in an effort to conceal a murder, for example, there is usually evidence to show that the fire was started deliberately. Alternatively the fire may have been started to enable a fraudulent insurance claim to be made, to destroy evidence of fraud, even to eliminate a business rival, or it may simply have been started to gratify the psychological appetite of a pyromaniac.

In most cases, setting a fire involves the use of some kind of accelerant to help the flames take hold. Fires tend to spread upward as well as outward, so the search for the start-point is usually focused on the lowest point of the burned-out area. There may be traces of gasoline or other flammable hydrocarbons, either lingering in the air or present in fabrics or surfaces on the edge of the area. These can be identified by laboratory analysis, either by being heated in water to liberate a

ABOVE Smoke patterning on the ceiling of a room in a burned-out building.

characteristic and identifiable scent, or by gas chromatography, which reveals the chemical composition of the hydrocarbons in question. This latter technique is so accurate that it can be used to differentiate between different makes and grades of gasoline. Each grade has a different chromatography "fingerprint" depending on the proportions of the different chemicals present. In some cases the chemical make-up can be measured so accurately that

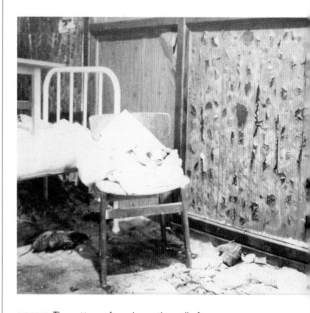

ABOVE The pattern of smoke on the wall of a room can help to show where a fire started and how it spread.

the gasoline can be traced to an individual gas station, or even to the fuel tank of a particular vehicle.

Piles of ash at the base of a fire may indicate where an arsonist piled material before lighting it. Any signs that the blaze had more than one point of origin strongly suggest that the blaze was deliberately started; evidence of breaking and entering can also point to arson. Where appropriate, investigators can check security or sprinkler systems to see whether they have been deliberately disabled. Where fraud or insurance swindles are suspected, investigators search carefully for the remains of goods or burned documents on the premises.

Where a fire is genuinely accidental, the cause is usually all too clear. The starting point may be found to be a fault in the building's electrical wiring, a gas leak, or a lighted cigarette carelessly disposed of. In other cases, evidence of a lightning strike or the presence of volatile materials stored near natural heat sources may show the cause.

ABOVE AND RIGHT A horrific fire at King's Cross station on the London subway system in 1987, which killed 31 people, was thought to have been started by a carelessly dropped cigarette setting light to an old wooden escalator.

In this reconstruction, the flames, which can just be seen in the top picture, have spread to cover the whole right-hand side of the escalator.

Within minutes, the wooden framework of the escalator is fully ablaze, preventing the trapped passengers using it as an escape route to the surface.

Explosive evidence

Explosions are caused by a combination of materials which, when detonated, set off a fast-burning reaction that produces gas. The gas causes the pressure inside the bomb's container to rise rapidly until the casing bursts and the pieces are blasted outward at high speed. Damage is inflicted and casualties caused not only by these fast-moving pieces but also by the blast effect of the expanding gases that are suddenly released from confinement and travel at speeds of up to 7,000 miles per hour.

Explosives are normally classified as one of two types, depending on how quickly the chemical reaction takes place. In "low" explosives, the reaction produces light, heat, and a subsonic pressure-wave flying outward in all directions from the detonation. In "high" explosives, the speed of the reaction is far greater, producing an almost instant build-up of heat and gases and a supersonic pressure-wave of destruction.

In most criminal cases involving explosives—excluding those organized by large, well-funded terrorist groups—the incendiary devices used are likely to be homemade. Most homemade explosives are low explosives, made from ingredients that are relatively easy to obtain. One traditional mixture, a black powder once used in muskets and pistols, is made from combining charcoal, sulfur and potassium or sodium nitrate. Others contain the essential combination of a fuel and an oxidant using ingredients as familiar as sugar and weed killer.

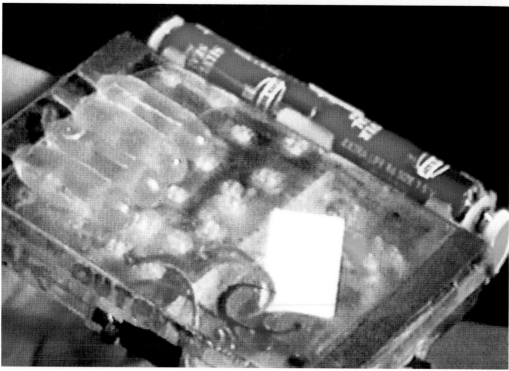

High explosives are more complex in their action. The most powerful of all, such as dynamite, TNT or RDX, are quite inert in themselves, and can be handled and even set on fire without exploding. For these, a primer is needed, a small charge of an explosive that is even more sensitive to heat or shock. Primer charges are usually detonated by blasting caps, which are triggered by lighting a safety fuse or applying an electric current. If the remains of one of these caps is found at the scene, it is usually safe to assume that the explosion was deliberately executed. The blasting caps of high explosives leave fragments that can be identified by sifting and then closely examining the debris found at the center of the explosion.

Searching for evidence

Even the most powerful and efficient explosives are not completely consumed in a deliberate detonation. Some residues inevitably remain at the scene, and forensic examiners now have a range of powerful tests at their disposal to reveal the presence and type of these traces.

In most cases, an explosion leaves a crater at the center of the blast, and debris is taken from this area for further tests. Fragments of softer materials such as wood, rubber or insulation may have absorbed traces of the explosives. Harder materials, such as metals, may have traces deposited on their surfaces.

OPPOSITE ABOVE The casing of a radio used to hide the bomb placed next to it.

OPPOSITE LEFT Part of the bomb used to destroy the PanAm Boeing Flight 103 747 over Lockerbie in 1988.

RIGHT Searching through the wreckage left when an El Al Boeing 747 freighter crashed into a block of flats near Amsterdam's Schiphol airport on October 4, 1992, a disaster that was eventually found to be caused by metal fatigue in the aircraft's mountings.

All these materials can be tested using chromatography equipment, and a portable machine that can be used at the scene itself is now commonly used. A vacuum pump collects vapors from suspect surfaces and passes them through its own high-speed gas chromatography equipment to identify their constituents. The device can detect commercial and military explosives, including the more sophisticated types of plastic explosives.

The detonator that sets off a low explosive is also usually homemade: an electrical detonator is sometimes linked to a battery

ABOVE Explosives investigation trucks at the scene of the Waco siege and shoot-out in Texas at the end of the 51-day standoff in April 1993.

ABOVE Part of the bomb used to blow the PanAm Boeing 747 airliner out of the sky over Lockerbie in 1988 (see p. 134).

through a device set to trigger the circuit. This might be an alarm clock, which allows the bomb to be set to go off at a particular time, or a mercury tilt switch, so that if the device is moved the circuit is completed and the bomb goes off. Many car bombs are wired to the vehicle's ignition, so the act of trying to start the engine sets off the explosion.

In some cases, analysis of the victims' bodies yields essential evidence. When a British European Airways Comet airliner was brought down in the eastern Mediterranean in

BELOW The victim of a Mafia assassination in Italy, lying next to his burning vehicle.

1967, the aircraft wreckage settled at the bottom of the sea and there was little of the plane left to show what had caused the disaster. Passengers' bodies floated to the surface, however, and autopsies were carried out. Forensic pathologists discovered that fragments of the bomb-casing had been driven deeply into the skin of one of the passengers. The site and severity of the wounds (together with the passenger manifest) enabled accident investigators to eventually determine the location of the bomb on the aircraft and the break-up sequence of the airliner, even though the airplane itself lay unrecovered on the sea bed.

Sabotage

Not all the evidence found at the scene of a fire or an explosion relates to the blaze, the detonation, the victims or the wreckage. The criminal may have broken into the area before setting the fire or planting the bomb, and left other pieces of evidence in the process. A tool such as a chisel or a screwdriver, when used to force open a door or window, leaves marks on the wood or metal that record the most minuscule shape and surface defects of the implement.

In cases such as vehicle sabotage, the criminal may have used saws and wire cutters, each of which leaves its signature impressions on the material being cut. Even knife scratches can give valuable evidence, especially if the suspect item is recovered and can be used to produce a test mark for comparison purposes. The pattern of marks resulting from the manufacture of the tool, together with any nicks and scratches acquired in its ordinary use, can be enormously helpful in ascertaining its origin and history.

TOP Wreckage and bodies in the aftermath of another Italian terrorist killing with a car bomb.

ABOVE This car was blown over by a bomb in a Mafia assassination in Palermo, Sicily.

Steven Benson

ABOVE Steven Benson at his trial in 1986.

Steven Benson came from a wealthy Florida family and expected to inherit a large sum of money on the death of his older relatives. On the morning of July 9, 1985, he arrived at his grandmother's home in Naples, Florida, to pick up some equipment to mark out a site for a new home. He loaded the family car, a 1978 Chevrolet Suburban, with stakes and plans, then he drove to a local store for coffee and rolls to bring back for the family breakfast.

Just before 9:00 AM, he and his mother, sister and adopted brother Scott went out to the car, ready to drive to the site. Finding that he had forgotten his tape measure, Steven threw the car keys to Scott and went back into the house. Scott climbed into the driving seat, turned the ignition key, and the car exploded in two separate but devastating blasts. Other than Steven, the only survivor was his sister Carol Lynn.

When forensic investigators arrived, they noted that Steven seemed remarkably calm considering that he had narrowly escaped being blown to pieces and had lost two members of his immediate family. As they searched the wreckage of the car, investigators' suspicions intensified. They found the remains of a bomb that had been made from a length of galvanized metal pipe, threaded at both ends and sealed with end-caps. One of the end-caps carried the letter G for its maker, Grinnell, and the other bore a U for Union Brand. Close to the site of the explosion,

BELOW Aerial view of the crime scene, with the wreckage in front of the Benson house in Naples, Florida.

fragments of four 1.5-volt batteries were found together with a manual switch and a piece of circuit board that was not part of the Suburban's electrical system.

Teams of investigators visited local hardware stores, junkyards and construction sites to check the sources of the pipes and end-caps. One store had sold two Union Brand end-caps four days before the explosion, and the description of the purchaser, who had been tall and heavily built matched that of Steven Benson. The sales tickets for the components were then chemically treated and revealed Steven Benson's palm print, proving that he had bought the bomb-making equipment.

On August 21, 1985, six weeks and a day after the fateful explosion, Benson was arrested. Almost a year later he was found guilty of the murders of his mother and brother. It emerged that Steven Benson had been stealing from his mother for some time. Having found him out, she was about to amend her will so that Steven would not inherit the ten million dollars he had been expecting. To prevent that from happening, he had been prepared to literally blow his family apart.

BELOW The twisted wreckage of the Chevrolet where Steven Benson's mother and brother died and (inset above) close-up of part of the wreckage.

Pan Am Flight 103

ABOVE Impact craters and debris from the crashed airliner in Lockerbie.

BELOW The nose and flight deck of the 747, found in a field more than two miles from the town.

At 6:25 PM (GMT) on December 21, 1988, A Pan American Boeing 747 originating in Frankfurt took off from London and headed for New York. Many of the two hundred and forty-three passengers on board were looking forward to spending the Christmas holiday with their families in the U.S. By 6:56 PM the airliner had reached its cruising altitude of 31,000 feet and was flying over southwestern Scotland following its Great Circle route toward the Atlantic. Seven minutes later, air-traffic controllers noticed with alarm that the airplane's echo had faded from the radar displays: it was replaced by several smaller, vanishing traces.

The disintegrating airliner fell out of the sky and hit the small Scottish town of Lockerbie, almost six miles below, with all the fury of an earthquake. One engine blew a crater fifteen feet deep in the northeastern part of the town, and the wing exploded in a fireball a quarter of a mile wide. Twenty-one local houses were destroyed in an impact registering 1.6 on the Richter scale; many more were badly damaged. Tragically, all two hundred and fifty-nine people aboard the aircraft died, as did eleven more on the ground.

The fact that the airplane victims were found to have suffered lung damage from violent decompression suggested that some catastrophic failure had made the aircraft disintegrate in the air. In order to establish the sequence of events leading to the disaster, investigators needed to collect as much of the wreckage as possible even though the debris was widely scattered.

Fragments had drifted in two trails of wreckage covering an area of almost a thousand square miles of northern England and part of Scotland. Nevertheless more than four million pieces were traced.

Eventually over ninety percent of the airplane's structure was recovered and used to reconstruct the plane in a huge hangar at a former army ammunition store.

At first the evidence seemed confusing. There had been no radio message giving a distress call. The flight data recorder showed that the control settings had been correct for normal

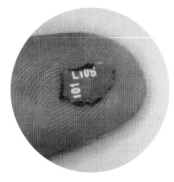

flight, and there was no sign of fatigue or corrosion in the engine or bodywork that could account for the airliner's disintegration.

Investigators examining the fragments found signs of explosive damage in luggage containers from the forward baggage hold: it seemed that a bomb had been detonated next to a container floor. Microscopic particles were found in the container walls and the aircraft skin panels, and a tiny piece of printed circuit board, part of a Toshiba radio cassette player, was found trapped in the container paneling. There were traces of Semtex (a plastic explosive), and residual fibers showed that the cassette player had been hidden inside a brown suitcase.

ABOVE Part of the detonator that set off the Lockerbie bomb.

The aircraft's disintegration appeared to have started when the bomb blew a small hole in the fuselage. The fuselage edges were then pulled back by the slipstream, the nose section tore away and the plane entered a steepening dive, breaking apart as it fell. In little more than ninety seconds, just 2.2 pounds of Semtex had blown apart a three-hundred-ton airliner, leading to the deaths of two hundred and seventy people.

Investigators started to focus on a detailed three-dimensional reconstruction of the part of the fuselage that held the bomb. Explosives experts assembled a series of identical devices, packed clothes in suitcases similar to those that were on the plane, and detonated them in identical luggage containers in an effort to establish the exact location of the device. The results showed that the case containing the bomb was loaded above the bottom layer of baggage in the container, which indicated that it was loaded onto the 747 at Frankfurt where transfer passengers boarded.

Forensic specialists found garment fibers in the fragments of the case. These were traced to clothes bought in Malta and flown to Frankfurt on the day of the crash. Investigations on Malta traced the purchase of the clothes to a Libyan who did not actually board the flight to London, though the baggage containing the clothes was accepted.

As a direct result of these findings, airlines have re-examined their policy on baggage loading, aiming to ensure that such a tragedy never happens again. Security checks on luggage have been intensified, and unaccompanied baggage can now be located before take-off. If passengers have checked in but fail to board a flight, their bags are removed from the hold.

BELOW Reconstruction of the baggage container that contained the bomb aboard the 747.

Research is currently being undertaken to see how airplanes can become more resistant to the forces of internal explosions. To guard against the possibility that terrorists will respond by making more powerful bombs, increasingly sensitive explosives detectors are being developed. These can reveal the presence of minute quantities of the chemicals used in incendiary devices by using variants of neutron activation analysis (see Chapter Twelve).

World Trade Center

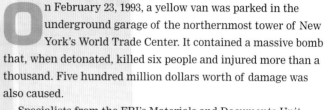

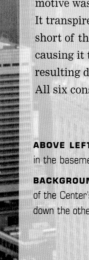

On February 23, 1993, a yellow van was parked in the underground garage of the northernmost tower of New York's World Trade Center. It contained a massive bomb that, when detonated, killed six people and injured more than a thousand. Five hundred million dollars worth of damage was also caused.

Specialists from the FBI's Materials and Documents Unit conducted detailed searches of the crime scene and managed to isolate trace evidence of urea nitrate. From the extent of the damage it was clear that at least twelve hundred pounds of the explosive was used.

Agents hunting for the bombers got an early break when an immigrant named Mohammad Salameh called at the rental office to claim back his $400 deposit on the rented Ryder van used in the bombing, which he said was stolen from him by Ramizi Ahmed Yousef, one of the principal conspirators, the day before. The police found Salameh's fingerprints on bomb-making chemicals once their investigation led them to a Jersey City apartment and a nearby storage shed used by Yousef as a bomb factory.

The fingerprints of Yousef and his chief conspirator, Eyad Izmoil, were found on chemicals and bomb-making manuals at the site, although the two men had left the U.S. on a flight from Kennedy Airport immediately after the bombing. A $2 million reward was posted, and two years later Yousef was arrested in Pakistan, after earlier sightings in Manila and Bangkok, and extradited to the U.S. to stand trial. Izmiol was later arrested in Jordan, and in November 1997 the two men were put on trial together with their follow plotters.

Six men with links to Arab countries were eventually tried and convicted of conspiracy to carry out the bombing. Their motive was to punish the U.S. for its continued support of Israel. It transpired that the carnage they caused had actually fallen far short of their intentions. Their aim was to blow up one tower, causing it to topple onto the other. Had they succeeded, the resulting death toll could have run into hundreds of thousands. All six conspirators were sentenced to life imprisonment.

ABOVE LEFT Investigators examine the rubble in the basement of the World Trade Center.

BACKGROUND The conspirators hoped that one of the Center's twin towers would collapse, bringing down the other, with a much greater loss of life.

The Oklahoma Bombing

ABOVE Bags of ammonium nitrate, commonly available as fertilizer in garden stores, and used in the Oklahoma bombing.

BELOW Devastation at the Alfred P. Murrah Federal Building in Oklahoma City after the bombing.

On April 19, 1995 the story of the Trade Center bomb was eclipsed by a much larger explosion—in the Alfred P. Murrah Federal Building in Oklahoma City, Oklahoma. One hundred and sixty-eight people died, many of whom were children attending a day-care center in the building.

Again, the forensic examiners' first priority was to collect and sift through tons of rubble in an effort to trace clues to the identity of the bombers. Almost 13,000 pieces of potential evidence were taken from the site of the explosion—including particles of metal removed from the bodies of the victims—and examined in detail. In fact one of the pieces of debris found in the earliest stages of the search gave investigators their most promising lead. A mangled piece of metal found close to the center of the blast was identified as part of a distorted truck axle. Close examination revealed a partial vehicle identification number that, when fed into the National Crime Insurance Bureau database, revealed that the axle belonged to a 1993 Ford truck. The truck belonged to Ryder Rentals of Miami, and investigators found that the vehicle had been hired out from a Ryder office in Junction City, Kansas.

Computer-enhanced artist's impressions were produced from descriptions given of the two people who hired the vehicle. Copies of the pictures were issued to more than a thousand agents from the FBI and the Bureau of Alcohol, Tobacco and Firearms, who began questioning staff at hotels, diners and gas stations between Junction City and Oklahoma City to see whether anyone remembered seeing or serving the suspects.

The manager of the Dreamland Hotel in Junction City thought one of the sketches resembled a man who stayed at his hotel and who drove a Ryder truck. The guest gave his name as Timothy McVeigh. The same sketch, which was also broadcast on television, prompted a one-time colleague of McVeigh's to call the FBI. He reported that he had been surprised by the vehemence with which McVeigh had reacted to news of the Waco shoot-out, in which FBI agents stormed the fortress of the Branch Davidian extreme religious sect.

Another lucky coincidence boosted the investigation at this point: initial attempts to locate McVeigh revealed that he was actually in custody already, having been arrested for an unrelated offense. The day after the bombing, Oklahoma State Trooper Charles D. Hangar spotted a yellow Mercury Marquis without a license plate on Interstate Highway 35. He asked the driver to pull over, and then found he was attempting to conceal a semiautomatic pistol. Details of the driver, who gave his name as Timothy McVeigh, were duly entered on the record.

Since McVeigh's name had been suggested by at least two sources in the FBI's inquiries into the bombing, it was keyed into the National Crime Information Center database. An immediate match was flagged, and inquiries revealed that the suspect was being held at Noble County Jail.

McVeigh's driver's license, which he had been carrying when he was arrested, gave a Michigan address. Local enquiries revealed that two brothers, Terry and James Nichols, had also been living there. Terry Nichols was eventually identified as suspect number two.

Forensic examiners believed that the explosives used in the bombing had been contained in fifty-gallon plastic barrels. Remains of barrels found at the bomb-site showed markings very similar to those found on empty barrels at Nichols' home. Furthermore, traces of the chemicals used in the explosives were found on the suspects' clothes.

Some of the assumptions made by forensic examiners concerning the type and amount of explosives used were later criticized, and some argued that the chemical traces found on the suspects' clothing might have come from a totally unrelated source. But the evidence linking the men to the truck that had contained the explosives proved unshakeable. Nichols was sentenced to life imprisonment and McVeigh, identified as the prime mover in the bombing, was sentenced to death.

McVeigh's attorneys appealed against his conviction on the grounds that the public climate at the time of the bombings prejudiced his right to a fair trial. The appeal was denied in March 1999. Nichols' appeal was quashed on October 12, 1999.

ABOVE Rescue teams sifting the wreckage of the building, searching for survivors.

BELOW Timothy McVeigh being taken by FBI agents from the Bonle County Courthouse in Perry, Oklahoma, where he had been arrested for a traffic offense and carrying a concealed firearm.

Unmasking the Criminal Frauds and Forgeries

ABOVE Testing a US currency bill under fluorescent light to reveal evidence of forgery.

The examination and testing of documents is an increasingly important area of forensic science. All kinds of clues to the identity of a criminal can be revealed by fragments of writing ranging from personal letters to ransom demands, or by printed documents from pawnbroker's receipts to airline or train tickets.

In other cases forged or altered letters, bank drafts, checks and similar financial documents can be profitable for a criminal if they can be passed off as genuine. Forensic specialists, however, can use a wide range of techniques to reveal even the most convincingly forged documents as fakes.

RIGHT Cleaning a medieval manuscript to ensure any tests carried out on it are accurate.

Other documents such as diaries and works of apparent historical significance are also tested to help prove their authenticity, usually by analysis of the writing and scientific testing of the paper and ink. Watermarks and

signatures can be checked to identify forgeries, and minute characteristics unique to individual typewriters or printers can be identified in pieces of text as a starting point for locating the machine that was used. Some techniques even allow deliberate corrections made at the time a document was created to be rendered transparent so that the underlying text is revealed.

Handwritten text

Most people are taught to write by copying a particular handwriting style. However, as individuals become more accustomed to writing and have to write more quickly, letters and words begin to acquire idiosyncrasies associated with that person's individual experience and coordination. Individual variations from the standard writing styles are the elements handwriting experts are most interested in, especially any differences that may be characteristic of, and so help identify, the writer.

Handwriting experts study in detail how particular letters have been formed in any given sample. For example, the letter "i" may be not be dotted, may be written without an upstroke, or may have one or more small "eyelets" where the movement of the pen changed direction in forming the letter. Not only do these characteristics show up throughout a particular sample of hand-written text, but in many cases they are

GALILEO GALILEI.
Date, 1609.
British Museum, Add. MS. 23,139

TOP Genuine handwriting of the Italian astronomer and physicist Galileo.

BELOW LEFT Researchers working on a computerized system for handwriting recognition.

present even when the writer is trying to conceal his or her identity, or attempting to imitate someone else's handwriting.

Another area of analysis involves the proportion or relative height of different letters. Even in an individual's ordinary handwriting, of course, variations do occur, but certain established ratios are usually consistent. For example, the ratio between the part of the letter "g" above the line to the overall height of the letter tends to remain the same in an individual writer, regardless of the writing style adopted.

The overall slant of the writing from the vertical is another fairly consistent factor. This

ABOVE Magnifying glass placed on a sheet of genuine Salvador Dali signatures, which can be used to authenticate unknown examples of the painter's work.

> visors in your agency become fully informed of the import
> of this Order. I am convinced that good personnel manage-
> ment can make a substantial contribution to the efficiency
> of the government.

> igations that are properly responsibilities of the
> States Government. Any arrangement proposed for the
> ion of this currency should include provisions designed
> as possible to avoid any windfall to speculators.

> of the President following appropriate discussions
> with yourself, Dr. Bush and the Director of Central
> Intelligence.

can range from thirty-five degrees to the right to as much as fifty degrees to the left in different styles, but it should be more or less consistent for a given person's hand. Experts measure the inclination using a transparent protractor, concentrating on the longest letters such as "f," "h," or "g."

Spacing of individual letters, words and lines is another respect in which writers' styles differ. In particular, a signature or a complete line of text tends to follow a consistent path for an individual. The baseline is either straight and level or angled or curved upward or downward or both. The presence or absence of connectors, the strokes that join letters in handwritten text, is another common individual variation.

Signatures

Perhaps no written words have as much forensic importance as signatures, and suspect examples are invariably checked against the genuine signature. Although each example of an individual's signature looks very similar, there are always subtle differences between them. If a suspect example, placed over a genuine example on a light box, looks completely identical, investigators automatically suspect forgery.

In order to establish whether or not a signature is genuine, forensic examiners gather as many copies of the genuine signature as possible. Ideally the collection includes casual scrawls as well as more formally written

LEFT President Harry S. Truman invariably placed his signature on typed documents close to the last lines of the text, as shown in the top and center examples. When checked by drawing a circle using the vertical stroke of the letter "T" in the signature as a radius, the forgery at the bottom is clearly too far from the text.

signatures, signatures written with different kinds of pens and, since handwriting can change with the passing of time, as many samples as possible dating from around the period when the suspect signature was supposed to have been written.

Although signatures made by one individual all differ slightly, there are certain features in each example that remain consistent; the placing of the signature relative to the typed or printed text in a letter, for example. Other similarities are associated with the actual shape of the signature rather than the formation of individual letters. By putting a sheet of tracing paper over a signature and marking the tops (or the bottoms) of each of the letters and then joining them up, a zigzag line is produced. Different genuine examples of the same signature all show a very similar line but a forgery, even one that seems convincing at first glance, often shows quite a different pattern from the original.

Other comparisons can be made by marking any gaps in the signature which, once again, produce a characteristic pattern. The baseline of the writing is another important element. Some forgers, concentrating on the formation of the letters, fail to notice the way in which the signature as a whole climbs or descends from left to right. The distinctive signature of Abraham Lincoln, for example, was characterized by a stepped baseline in which the initial "A" and the final "ln" lay on different levels from the rest of the name—an idiosyncrasy missed by several would-be forgers of his day.

Microscopic examination can show further discrepancies between a genuine signature, usually written quickly and confidently, and a forgery, where the writer took care to make the shape as convincing as possible. A microscope reveals any breaks in the lines, tremors, patching (where badly-shaped letters were corrected), or any pencil tracing and eraser marks made when the signature was transferred from a genuine example.

ABOVE Abraham Lincoln and his genuine signature, showing the characteristic three steps of the baseline, a feature often missed by forgers.

Disguised writing

Not all criminals try to imitate the writing of others. Some try to disguise their own writing to avoid revealing their identity. There are several common ways of doing this: some would-be forgers change the direction in which the letters slant, others change the size of the letters, print in block capitals, or even write with the other hand. Writing quickly or slowly, deliberately misspelling words or trying to copy another handwriting style are other tricks of the trade.

Many of the most obvious changes are ignored by experts when comparing disguised

ABOVE W. F. Thomas (left), alias William Henry Podmore, hanged in April 1930 for the murder of Vivian Messiter (right).

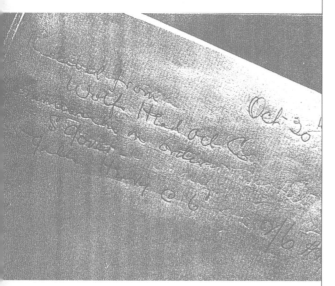

ABOVE Impression of handwriting on a receipt book, found at the scene of the murder of Vivian Messiter in Southampton, England in January 1929, when viewed in oblique light revealed the handwriting and signature of W. F. Thomas an alias of his murderer, William Henry Podmore.

writing with a sample produced by a suspect. Smaller, more subtle signs of individuality, such as the forming of individual letters, are more difficult for the writer to eliminate. Other clues are the way in which the writer starts or ends a particular letter each time it appears.

One way of confirming the identity of a writer is by locating the origin of the

document in question. A search of a suspect's home or office may uncover partially destroyed drafts, or examination of the remaining pages of a notepad or the desk blotter may show pressure marks of the pen where a document was written. Modern forensic science can bring powerful techniques to bear on both these possibilities. Fragments of torn-up and burned documents can be reassembled and read by photographing them under infrared light, or alternatively under light that is reflected at different angles off the burned surface of the paper to produce the greatest possible contrast between the writing and the scorched background.

When an imprint is left on paper that was underneath the document at the time of writing, as in the case of successive pages of a notepad, for example, electrostatic detection can provide a lot of useful information. Each page of the notepad is placed in turn over an electronically charged wire mesh and tightened against it using a shrink-wrap technique. A form of photocopier toner is then applied which clings to the parts of the document that were pressed down by the action of the pen on the top sheet. These came into closest contact with the charged mesh, so picking up an electrostatic charge. This technique is so sensitive that images can be retrieved from several pages torn off the pad in succession. It is even possible to reconstruct the order in which the pages lay in the original pad, and therefore the order in which different sections of text were written.

Typewriting and printing

The introduction of typewriters and computer printers forced forensic examiners to meet new challenges in identifying the origins of machine-written documents. Manual typewriter text analysis is based on the fact that different pressures on the keys and differing wear on individual letter keys eventually build up a series of discrepancies that are distinguishable in text typed on any particular machine. Some letters become displaced upward or downward from the line of text, others skew from the vertical as type bars become twisted. Some letters become broken or indistinct with use, all of which helps in identifying a suspect machine.

Developments in typing and printing technology have tended to reduce the value of this kind of analysis. The introduction of electric typewriters, in which even pressure is applied to all key strokes, reduced variations in the weight with which different letters were typed, though faults in the mechanism can replace the action of the typist's fingers in creating new inconsistencies. The availability of golf-ball typewriters, which allow a whole font to be changed by substituting another ball in a matter of seconds, also complicates the experts' task. But perhaps the advent of

ABOVE AND ABOVE LEFT Typebars of a typewriter with raised and reversed letters and symbols, can become worn and displaced with use, producing characteristic misalignments like the raised figures of the date in the sample of text.

computer-controlled printers has provided the greatest obstacle to those seeking the individual quirks and variations that identify a particular machine.

In the first word-processors, output was often delivered on a daisy-wheel printer, where the type was set on bars that formed the spokes of a wheel. These were susceptible to wear and tear in a similar way to typewriters, and because the mechanisms of both golf-ball and daisy-wheel machines can become slightly misaligned with use, documents printed on a particular machine could still be identified with some accuracy.

Since then, the increasing popularity of ink-jet, bubble-jet and laser printers has tended to eliminate these useful inconsistencies. Other ways of linking the author to the document have had to be found, such as tracing the original word-processor files on the hard disk of the computer, for example. Although the writer may have taken care to delete the files in question, they can often still be retrieved by computer experts who know how and where to search for them.

Inks and papers

Elaborate forgeries of printed documents can be extremely convincing to casual inspection, but are often revealed as counterfeit when tests are carried out on the paper or the ink used. Modern inks fall into four basic types. Most black inks contain dye material and iron salts in a suspension of gallic or tannic acid. India ink, or carbon-black ink, is made from a suspension of carbon particles in gum Arabic, and a whole range of colored inks is made using synthetic dyes with different polymers and acids. Ball-point pens use inks made with synthetic dyes or insoluble pigments in a range of solvents and additives.

ABOVE The English poet Lord Byron with a genuine sample of his handwriting.

LEFT Testing inks using chromatography to reveal their exact composition.

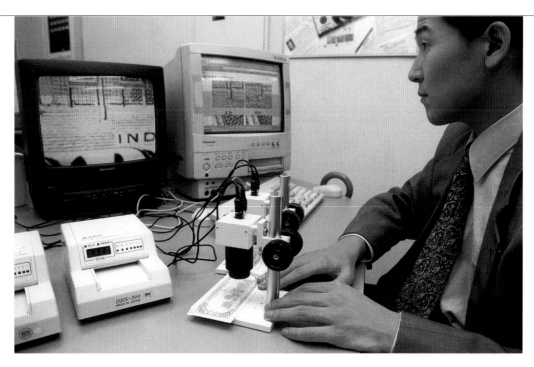

Within these basic types there are thousands of variations. Each can be isolated by using methods such as spectrometry or thin-layer chromatography. The U.S. Bureau of Alcohol, Tobacco and Firearms has a database of more than 3000 different ink chromatograph traces that can help to identify a particular ink composition.

Paper too can be classified by the different materials used in its manufacture. Some papers have particular watermarks, others are made from synthetic fibers or have optical brightening agents like fluorocarbons added to make them whiter and less transparent for high-quality color printing. Papers also differ in the surface treatment used to prepare them for printing: some are hot-rolled, others treated with size, synthetic resins or starch.

Specialists are often able to ascertain the date when a particular paper or type of ink was originally introduced, and this can reveal an otherwise convincing historical document as a forgery. A document once thought to be an original manuscript by the English poet Byron was found to have a watermark showing the paper was manufactured in 1834, ten years after his death.

Some forgers attempt to increase the value of postage stamps to collectors by faking the cancellation stamps, and many attempt the most difficult forgeries of all by producing counterfeit currency. Here, of course, the papers and the printed designs used by mints are chosen specifically to make the forger's task as difficult as possible. Even where the reproduction of the printed design is perfect to the naked eye, techniques such as

microspectrophotometry can reveal the absorption spectrum of the ink used in individual printed lines, making it a simple matter to distinguish between genuine and forged notes.

So numerous and varied are the obstacles facing the would-be currency forger that in one classic case, the criminals thought of an original twist to simplify their task. In 1924, using inside knowledge, they forged "official" letters to a British printing firm that produced Portugal's currency notes. These letters ordered a special printing of five-hundred-

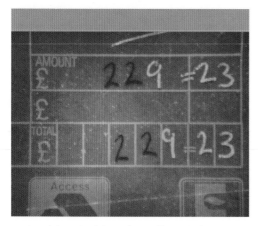

ABOVE A tungsten-halogen lamp with a set of filters reveals the luminescence of the ink, and a transmitted light source shows masked or obliterated text on a document.

BELOW The original check (top) is altered by the forger to pay a much larger amount (bottom) by a few additional pen strokes.

escudo notes for the Portuguese colony of Angola. The notes, according to the letter, were to be normal Portuguese currency, to be overprinted "Angola" by the Portuguese themselves. The notes were printed, collected by the criminals using forged letters of authorization, and then used to buy shares and foreign currency.

The ingenious twist to this case was that the notes were perfect, and the crime came to light only when a check was made on the number of five-hundred-escudo notes in circulation. The check was ordered after a batch of genuine notes had been printed with the same serial numbers as those ordered by the criminals. Even then the main culprit managed to delay his trial by five years by producing more forged letters, this time implicating the governor and directors of the Bank of Portugal in the deception and portraying himself as an innocent scapegoat.

Changing checks and drafts

Many criminals avoid the need for complex and difficult forgeries by altering existing documents such as checks and bank drafts, either by changing the name of the payee or by increasing the amount involved. Such changes often involve erasing one or more characters on the existing document by scratching away the surface layer of the paper, and then typing or writing over the alteration. Microscopic analysis usually reveals the signs of such an alteration when the document is lit from one side to highlight changes in the surface layers.

In other cases, criminals erase existing characters by using a chemical agent. This works by reacting with the ink to produce a colorless product, but the part of the paper to which the chemical is added reveals its secret when examined under infrared or ultraviolet lighting. Even if a skillful forger does not remove any of the existing text or figures and simply adds to them, examiners can use a

technique called infrared luminescence to reveal these later alterations.

By shining blue-green light onto the document, then photographing it using infrared-sensitive film, investigators can highlight differences in the luminescent properties of the inks. Illuminating the document with infrared light before the infrared photography also shows discrepancies in the capacity of different inks to absorb infrared light. In either case, the alterations appear different from the original writing, making it clear that the document has been tampered with.

In the Clifford Irving case (see Chapter Fifteen) the criminal did not even have to alter the check, which had been made out to the subject of a so-called authorized biography. The check was given to Irving for transmission to the reclusive billionaire Howard Hughes, but Irving's wife opened a bank account in the name of Helga R. Hughes. The check, which was made out to H. R. Hughes, was paid into the account, therefore, without any alterations being necessary.

RIGHT The forgery is revealed using infrared luminscence.

The Hitler Diaries

ABOVE Gerd Heidemann with some of the volumes he claimed were the diaries of Adolf Hitler.

In 1981, twenty-seven volumes of handwritten text believed to be the diaries of Adolf Hitler were bought by the German publishing firm, Grüner and Jahr, together with a previously undiscovered third volume of Hitler's *Mein Kampf*, for a sum equivalent to two million dollars. The story was that the volumes had been smuggled out of Berlin in the last days of World War Two, but the airplane carrying them had crashed in what was later Communist East Germany. The papers had fallen into the hands of a collector of Nazi documents whose brother had been an East German general. The collector had brought the documents to Gerd Heidemann, a journalist on the staff of the German news magazine *Stern*, which was also published by Grüner and Jahr.

Naturally the documents were checked for authenticity against known samples of Hitler's handwriting. Two experts were brought in to carry out the checks, Max Frei-Sultzer, former head of the Zürich police forensic science department, and Ordway Hilton, a specialist in document verification from Landrum in South Carolina. Both men, together with another German police documents expert, confirmed that the texts had been written by the same person, which was actually true. The diaries had been forged by a small-time criminal named Konrad Kujau, who

BACKGROUND The Remington typewriter on which Hitler had written *Mein Kampf*.

RIGHT Hitler's dedication and signature on a first edition of the book.

156

LEFT Konrad Kujau, the forger of the diaries, appearing in court with samples of his handiwork.

had also succeeded in forging the sample used to check the diaries' authorship!

The truth was revealed by West German police and government forensic tests. Instead of checking the handwriting, they concentrated on the paper and ink used in the diaries. After testing the paper under ultraviolet light, they found it contained a whitening agent that had first been introduced in 1954. The threads attaching the official-looking seals to the volumes contained viscose and polyester, materials that had been developed since the war, and none of the four different types of ink used had been available when the diaries were supposed to have been written. Finally, the evaporation of chloride from the ink was tested to establish how long the ink had been on the paper—the results showed that the documents had been written less than a year before the tests were carried out.

BELOW At a press conference, Gerd Heidemann denies that he had set out to cheat *Stern* magazine with the forged diaries.

The Diary of Jack the Ripper

An unemployed scrap-dealer from Liverpool, England, named Michael Barrett, claimed in 1991 to have been given a Victorian scrapbook that appeared to contain the diaries of Jack the Ripper, the notorious nineteenth-century serial killer. Barrett claimed that he had been given the scrapbook by a friend, Tony Devereux, who had since died. Rumors linked Devereux with workers who had carried out rewiring at a house formerly owned by the alleged author of the diaries, Liverpool businessman James Maybrick, who had died of arsenic and strychnine poisoning in 1889.

A series of tests has since been carried out on the diary, even though Barrett himself later claimed to have forged it, but then retracted his confession. One senior London psychiatrist found the variation in handwriting and the phrases used could be consistent with a potential serial killer. Again the tests were designed to analyze two distinct elements: the handwriting and the materials. Comparisons were made between the handwriting in the diary and that used in Maybrick's will, to show whether or not they could have been written by the same person; the paper and ink were analyzed to see whether their make-up was consistent with that used during Maybrick's lifetime.

ABOVE James Maybrick—Murder victim, or serial murderer?

BELOW One of the letters which was sent to the police at the time of the Ripper Murders, and which was supposed to have been written by the killer himself.

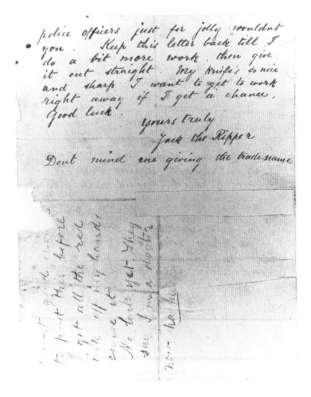

Scientific opinion remains divided. Handwriting analysis by the former forensic document expert for the Chicago Police Department concluded that the handwriting differed from the signature on Maybrick's marriage license and that on his will. But there are those who believe the diary reveals details that would be unknown to a forger, and some contend that the will was the faked document. Such a possibility was indeed aired at the time of Maybrick's death, since the will disinherited his own children. Believers also argue that Maybrick's formal signature is too small a sample to use for objective comparison.

On the paper and ink used in the diary, opinion is similarly split. Tests carried out by Dr. Nicholas Eastaugh, a document specialist who worked for the auction house Christie's as well as London museums and art galleries, indicated that the ink could have been right for the period. Analysis of the paper showed no trace of any modern additives. But Michael Barrett in his confession claimed to have bought an antique Victorian scrapbook and a bottle of "Victorian ink" to carry out his forgery, which he composed with the help of detailed library research. To confuse the picture still further, one American document specialist referred to an ink solubility test carried out in the U.K. which "appeared to show the ink was barely dry on the pages." For the moment it is not clear whether the Ripper diaries are authentic or not.

BELOW The envelope sent to the Central News agency contained a letter from the Ripper (background picture).

Fingerprints and Footprints

ABOVE Individual identifier—a false-color computer graphics image of a human fingerprint.

The fact that every living person has a unique pattern of ridges and depressions on the tips of their fingers is one of the founding principles of forensic science. It offers not only the possibility of positively identifying an individual victim or criminal, but also of proving the presence of a suspect at the scene of a crime.

The principle was recognized three thousand years ago in ancient China, where it was common for legal contracts to be endorsed by the fingerprints of the parties involved. The custom was also adopted by the Japanese. In the nineteenth century, an Englishman named William Herschel working in the Indian Civil Service introduced a similar practice; contracts were "signed" by the print of the signatory's right hand, which had been inked by being pressed on the ink pad normally used for rubber stamps.

The technique of using fingerprints as a way of identifying individuals was developed by another British expatriate, Dr. Henry Faulds, a Scot working in a Tokyo hospital. He was involved in a case where a thief had left a fingerprint on a whitewashed wall. When a suspect was identified, Fauld noticed that the patterns of ridges and whorls on the suspect's

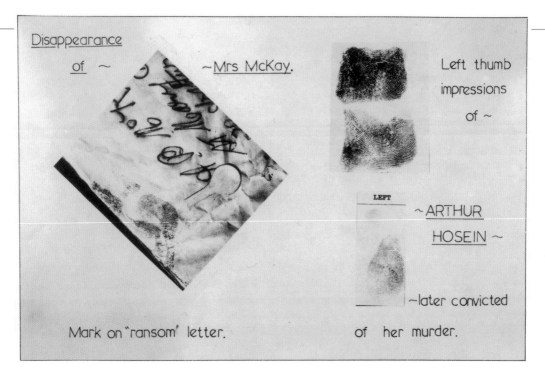

Disappearance

of ~ ~Mrs McKay.

Left thumb
impressions
of ~

LEFT

~ARTHUR
HOSEIN ~

~later convicted

Mark on 'ransom' letter.   of her murder.

fingers were quite different from those left in the whitewash. When an alternative suspect was apprehended, his prints were taken and the patterns compared—this time they matched perfectly.

Faulds published his conclusions in a scientific paper in 1880, and even volunteered to fund a fingerprint bureau at Scotland Yard, London's police headquarters, hoping that a practical method for identifying criminals could be developed. At the time, the "vital measurement" teachings of Bertillon (see Chapter One) still seemed to point the way forward, and Fauld's offer was declined. What Scotland Yard needed was an accurate and reliable method of classifying prints, as well as practical illustration that fingerprint evidence could prove an individual's identity with greater certainty than Bertillon's methods could.

Thanks to the work of Sir Francis Galton in England, Edward Henry in India and Juan Vucetich in Argentina, it became possible to classify and describe prints in such a way that matches could be reliably confirmed or rejected. The superiority of fingerprint evidence over Bertillon's "vital measurement" records was confirmed, in the United States at

TOP Fingerprints of Arthur Hosein, convicted of the kidnap and murder of Mrs Muriel McKay in England in 1968, matched with prints on the ransom note.

MIDDLE Fingerprint comparator with a glass magnifying lens and a cool-white fluorescent light source.

BOTTOM Recording fingerprints on a standard form.

least, by the case of a prisoner named Will West who arrived at Fort Leavenworth Prison, Kansas, to serve his sentence. The prison records showed there was already another prisoner in the penitentiary named William West, totally unconnected with the first Will West. The two men looked alike and their records, according to the Bertillon system, were identical. The only way they could be reliably distinguished was by their fingerprints.

Classifying fingerprints

Prints are classified by the pattern of ridges on the surface of the skin. At different points on the fingertip, these ridges come to an end, or divide, or cross; and the resulting complex

ridge patterns are different in every single individual. The general ways in which the ridges are arranged follow a series of recognizable patterns which allow prints to be systematically classified so that a search for a match can begin with general characteristics, then proceed to more detailed points of resemblance.

Two-thirds of the human population, for example, have ridge patterns that form loops. These are classified as "radial" (from the

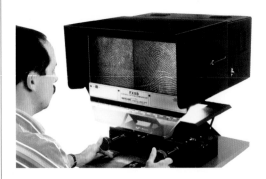

ABOVE Another type of fingerprint comparator, which presents two prints side-by-side for detailed matching under high magnification.

LEFT AND BELOW Fingerprint classifications including different types of loops and arches.

Ulnar loop

Central pocket loop

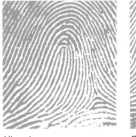
Plain whorl

Double loop

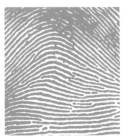
Plain arch

Tented arch

Double loop

Accidental

Tented arch

Radial loop

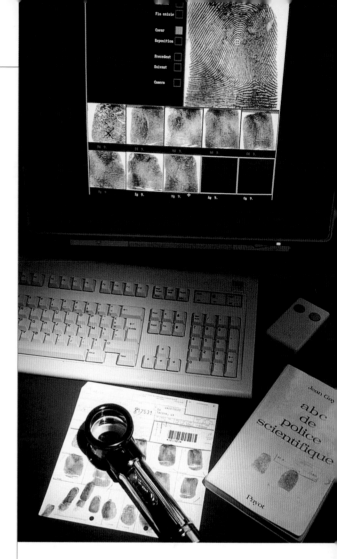

radius bone of the forearm) if the loops open toward the little-finger side of the hand; "ulnar" (from the ulna bone) if they open toward the thumb. The center of the loop is called the core, and the triangular pattern where the outermost looped ridge lines meet the horizontal ridge-line pattern running across the base of the fingertip is called the "delta."

Almost one-third of the population has ridge patterns in whorls, which can be further split into plain whorls, double loops, central-pocket loops and accidental loops. Approximately one person in twenty has ridge patterns arranged in arches, which are described as plain arches if they follow a smooth, wavelike pattern, or tented arches if they end in a sharper point at the center.

Henry's system, and the later development of this system used by the FBI, splits the possible variants into 1,024 coded groups to simplify searches. Each of an individual's ten prints is assigned a numerical value. First of all, the prints are arranged as a double row in the following sequence:

Right index finger   Right ring finger   Left thumb   Left middle finger   Left little finger

Right thumb   Right middle finger   Right little finger   Left index finger   Left ring finger.

Each print is then given a value depending on the pattern of the print and the finger in question. If either of the fingers at the beginning of each row (the right index finger or the right thumb) has a whorl pattern, it scores a value of sixteen. If either finger of the second pair (the right ring finger or the right middle finger) has a whorl, it scores eight. The third, fourth and last pairs score four, two and one respectively if either of them has a whorl; any finger that has no whorl pattern is given a zero score.

The scores on each row are then added up and one further point added to each unless all the fingers on that row have whorls. The result is presented as a fraction, such as 14/8 or 16/9,

ABOVE The handheld digitizer at the bottom of the picture is used to transfer old paper copies of criminals' fingerprints from existing records into data which can be fed into computer databanks.

which provides an overall class figure, and this acts as a starting point in any search for a matching print.

This type of pattern recognition is an ideal application for computers, which can scan and store a given fingerprint as a digital pattern, taking account of the type and location on the print of each individual feature. These automated fingerprint identification systems (A.F.I.S.) can search a file of hundreds of thousands of digital print records for a match in less than a second, and offer a series of close matches for final scrutiny by a fingerprint expert. The computer also makes it feasible to

find a match for a single print found at a crime scene, even though the original FBI formula was based on a knowledge of all ten prints.

Computer-based storage systems also allow prints to be compared on high-resolution monitors and can enhance poor-quality or smudged prints to produce a sharp image. In addition, data can be exchanged with other A.F.I.S. systems and prints can be sent across the world to be compared or matched with locally obtained prints.

Revealing and recording prints

The fingerprints searched for at crime scenes fall into three main categories: visible, plastic or latent. Visible prints are the easiest to spot, being those made by fingers that have been in contact with a marker such as wet paint, ink, or blood. Plastic prints are made by the fingers pressing on a material like soap, wax, or putty which retains the image of the finger-tip ridges. Latent prints, however, the most common type, are also the hardest to see and need to be exposed before examination.

Latent fingerprints are made when the natural oils and perspiration present between the fingertip ridges are transferred to a surface by touch. The method used to reveal such minute traces

depends on the type of surface being tested. Hard and non-absorbent surfaces like glass, painted wood, tiles or metal are usually dusted with fingerprint powder which sticks to the traces of oil and perspiration left by the fingertip. The powder is made in different colors so that investigators can select the one that provides the sharpest contrast with the surface being dusted. Fine carbon powder is used to reveal latent prints on light-colored surfaces, while aluminum powder reveals prints on dark surfaces. Fluorescent powder can also be used, and this is photographed under ultraviolet light so that the fluorescing latent print will stand out even against the most brightly colored or patterned surface.

Soft or porous surfaces such as cloth or paper can yield fingerprint evidence through the use of chemical methods. The oldest method is iodine fuming. The article is examined by being placed inside an enclosed cabinet with iodine crystals and then heated. The iodine vapor given off by the crystals combines with the traces of the print in a chemical reaction that leaves a visible pattern.

and a fluorescent dye. These wands can be used to test a suspect area that includes both porous and non-porous surfaces.

One of the latest techniques for revealing latent prints involves illuminating them with laser light, which causes chemicals in human perspiration to fluoresce in darkness. Different chemicals are used to intensify this effect. Alternative types of lasers or other high-intensity light sources such as quartz or xenon arc lamps can be set up relatively easily in most locations. In all these cases, the prints have to be placed on permanent record by being photographed or "lifted" using adhesive tape or plastic sheet to attract the fingerprint powder and preserve the all-important patterns.

Other chemical methods use a ninhydrin spray that forms a purple-blue color when combined with the traces of amino acids in human perspiration; or silver nitrate, which reacts with the salt in perspiration to form silver chloride, which in turn is revealed under ultraviolet light.

A newer technique is known as superglue fuming because it relies on cyanoacrylate ester, the active ingredient in this type of very strong, quick-acting adhesive. The fumes can be applied by heating the object in a closed cabinet, as with iodine fuming, or by filling the whole of a closed space, such as the interior of an automobile, with fumes to reveal every latent print. Hand-held wands have also been developed that heat a small cartridge containing a mixture of the active ingredient

ABOVE A fiberglass latent print brush and latent print-lifting tape.

Fingerprinting the dead

Fingerprinting has now become a standard part of autopsy procedure, effected after all other possible trace evidence has been removed from the fingertips and fingernails. If some time has elapsed since the death of a victim, "reconstructive" procedures have to be undertaken to ensure a clear set of prints.

Taking fingerprints from dead bodies is usually carried out when rigor mortis has passed off and after the body has been kept in cold storage. Bodies that are badly decomposed sometimes have to have the hands, or occasionally individual fingers, removed to aid the taking of the prints. Mummified bodies may need to have the fingertips softened by being soaked in a mixture of glycol, lactic acid and distilled water, sometimes for several weeks, before prints can be taken.

The most difficult subjects are those in which the skin has been softened by damp or immersion in water. In some cases glycerine or liquid wax has to be injected into the fingertip from below the joint. If the damage to the tissues is more extensive, the skin can be stripped away from the hand to be mounted on a surgical glove for prints to be taken. In one case in 1933 in Australia, the unidentified body

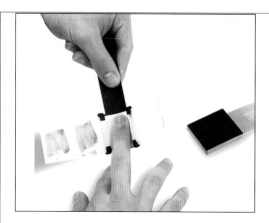

of a murder victim was found in the Murrumbidgee River with one hand missing and the other badly mutilated. The discovery of the outer skin of the missing right hand further along the river bank enabled this technique to be used to retrieve the prints. As a result the victim was identified as a down-and-out named Percy Smith, and eventually a fellow vagrant named Edward Morey was convicted of his murder.

Other identifiers

The patterns of the ridged skin on the palms of the hands and the soles of the feet are also unique to each individual, but prints of these are not usually kept for record purposes. Nonetheless, if a barefoot print or a palm print

BELOW Taking the fingerprints of a corpse.

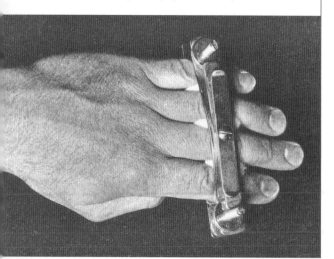

ABOVE A postmortem record strip holder for fingerprinting the dead.

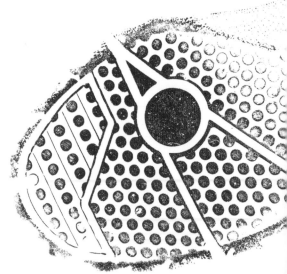

is retrieved at the scene of a crime, potential suspects can be eliminated if their prints do not match. In some countries, the barefoot prints of new babies are used to provide positive proof of individual identity in maternity hospitals, since babies' fingerprints are too small for their features to be easily identified.

Other individual features are used to help identify faces from security-camera recordings. The basic proportions of the face can be computer-processed to enable them to be

compared with photographs of a suspect taken from different angles and perspectives. The shape of the ears is one highly individual characteristic, since this varies from one person to the next and remains virtually the same for the whole of a subject's lifetime.

ABOVE A complete shoe print from an athletic shoe showing individual intricacies of the pattern.

RIGHT Comparing a heel print photograph taken at a crime scene with the shoe of a suspect.

Thomas Jennings

BACKGROUND Thomas Jennings, whose fingerprints in wet paint at the crime scene resulted in his conviction for murder.

The Hiller family lived on Chicago's West 104th Street. In the early hours of September 19, 1910, Mrs. Hiller woke her husband Clarence and told him the gas lamp outside their daughter's bedroom was not burning properly. He got up to check and met a stranger on the landing. Hiller challenged the intruder, the two men fought and both fell down the stairs. The intruder then fired two shots and fled, leaving Clarence Hiller dying on the floor.

Neighbors arrived to help and the police were called, though a suspect had already been arrested less than a mile from the murder scene. Four off-duty officers had seen a man running as if evading pursuers, constantly turning to look behind him. When they stopped and searched him, they found he was carrying a loaded revolver. His name was Thomas Jennings and there were bloodstains on his clothing which he claimed had been made when he fell from a streetcar.

When officers searched the scene of the murder, they found three unused cartridges close to Mr. Hiller's body and some traces of sand and gravel at the foot of the daughter's bed, but these proved less significant than the fingerprints found in the kitchen. The day before his murder, Clarence Hiller had painted some railings next to the window through which the killer had gained access. The paint was still wet and had preserved a perfect set of four fingerprints from the intruder's left hand.

The Chicago police force was one of the first in the United States to recognize the value of fingerprinting. When Jennings' prints were compared with those at the Hiller house, they proved a perfect match. The case against Jennings was reinforced by a match between the bullets found in Clarence Hiller's body and test bullets fired from Jennings' gun, and he was found guilty of murder. His attorneys appealed on the grounds that fingerprint evidence was not admissible, but the verdict was confirmed on appeal. Jennings, the first felon in the United States to have been convicted on fingerprint evidence, was sentenced to death on December 21, 1911, and on a later date hanged.

The Shark Arm Case

On April 25, 1935, a tiger shark at Sydney's Coogee Beach aquarium appeared to suffer a violent fit, thrashing backward and forward in the water. The cause of the shark's discomfort finally became clear when it managed to regurgitate the obstruction—a human arm.

Forensic experts found that the arm was muscular and well developed as a result of regular exercise. An unusual tattoo of two boxers fighting was still visible. An early priority was to take fingerprints, even though the skin of the hand was in a very fragile condition. By removing the skin in small flakes and reassembling the fingertips piece by piece, the police managed to obtain the prints they needed to identify the owner of the arm. The tattoo alone had not proved enough of a distinguishing characteristic, even among missing persons, to provide the lead the police needed.

The arm was eventually traced to one James Smith, a former boxer with criminal connections who had vanished from his home on April 8 that year, telling his wife he had rented a cottage for a fishing holiday with a friend called Patrick Brady. Brady, who had links to drug trafficking, was arrested but denied all responsibility for Smith's death, casting suspicion instead on the local boatbuilder, Reginald Holmes.

Close examination of the arm showed that it had been hacked from Smith's body by a sharp knife, not bitten off by the shark's teeth, and that this had happened some time after Smith's death. At the rented cottage, police checked the owner's inventory and found that a trunk, a length of rope, a mattress and three mats were missing. They assumed Smith had been killed in the cottage and his body cut up on the spot. They also assumed that most of the body parts had been crammed into the trunk but they discovered that the remainder, including his arm, had been roped to the outside of the trunk before it was dumped at sea.

In spite of all these promising leads, the murderer was never found. Holmes claimed Brady had carried out the murder, but Holmes himself was murdered before he could testify at the inquest. Brady was still the prime suspect in the Smith killing, but he had still been in custody at the time of Holmes'.death. Although both the motive and perpetrator remain unknown, the extraordinary sequence of events leading to the identification of the victim earned this case a unique place in the history of forensic science.

ABOVE The arm of James Smith, disgorged by a captured Tiger Shark in a Sydney aquarium, and showing the tattoo of a boxer.

ABOVE The murderer of James Smith (right) has never been found.

Peter Griffiths

June Anne Devaney was a three-year-old patient in the children's ward of Queen's Park Hospital in Blackburn, England, in 1948. She was recovering from a bout of pneumonia. During the early hours of May 15 the child was abducted; less than two hours after the alarm was raised, the search revealed her fearfully battered body lying dead in the hospital grounds. She had been raped and there were teeth marks on her skin, but there was no other evidence to help identify her killer.

The police concentrated on the ward from which she had been taken. They checked every footprint on the polished floor and discovered a set of prints of stockinged feet that could not have belonged to any of the nurses. The tracks led first to a trolley at the end of the ward, from which a bottle of sterile water had been taken, then to the child's bed. The bottle had been left under the bed. The police then checked every print on the bottle and, having painstakingly eliminated those belonging to the hospital staff, were left with one single set: those of the killer.

The place where the child's body had been left suggested to police that the culprit was someone with local knowledge. They undertook the daunting task of fingerprinting every male over the age of sixteen in the whole city area—more than 46,000 men. Almost eight weeks later, having completed that search and checked all local records, they had still not found a match.

At that time, some aspects of wartime rationing were still in force in Britain and all adults had to be issued with ration books. The electoral registers, which had been used for the fingerprint campaign, were cross-checked against registers of ration-book holders. Police were surprised to find that these second registers contained details of more that two hundred men who had not appeared on the first lists. Checking was resumed and, on August 11, police found that the prints of subject number 46,253, a twenty-two-year-old Blackburn flour mill worker called Peter Griffiths, provided a perfect match.

BACKGROUND A record from the mass fingerprinting campaign.

LEFT Entrance to the hospital ward from which June Anne Devaney was abducted.

RIGHT Fingerprints on a glass bottle made visible by dusting with fingerprint powder.

BOTTOM A policewoman at the headquarters of Blackburn CID hands over fingerprint record forms to a plainclothes police officer working on the case.

Peter Griffiths was identified by the world's first mass fingerprinting campaign. Other evidence linking him to June Devaney's terrible murder was discovered by matching fibers from the child's nightgown with some found on his clothes and by fitting his stockinged feet to the prints found on the hospital floor. His niece had been a patient in the hospital at the same time as his victim. Though initially he denied any involvement, he finally confessed, was found guilty at trial and hanged in November 1948.

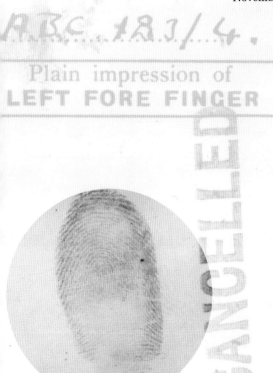

Ted Bundy

ABOVE, LEFT TO RIGHT Three of Bundy's alleged victims: Laura Aime, Debbie Kent, and Melissa Smith who all disappeared in 1974 in Utah.

BELOW Ted Bundy appears in court, restrained by handcuffs and a leg brace.

Serial killer Theodore (Ted) Bundy killed more than forty young women in a spree spanning almost a decade. The killings began in 1969 in California and spread through Oregon and Washington and into Utah and Colorado. The murder victims all shared certain physical characteristics, and when the different police forces compared notes on suspects they found Bundy's name was another recurring theme—but none had proof of anything more sinister than his presence in the vicinity of the crimes.

Bundy made his first mistake in Salt Lake City in November 1974 when he tried to abduct 18-year-old Carol DaRonch by claiming to be a plainclothes police officer. She climbed into his car, but when he produced a pair of handcuffs and tried to attack her with a crowbar, she managed to struggle free and escape. She reported the incident, but it was not until August the following year that a Salt Lake City police officer noticed a Volkswagen driver behaving suspiciously, and stopped him. A crowbar and handcuffs were found in the car, prompting an association with the attempted abduction of Carol DaRonch. She identified Bundy, and he was sentenced to fifteen years' imprisonment for the attack.

Unfortunately, while being taken to Colorado to be charged with another murder in June 1977, Bundy escaped. He was recaptured after eight days, but within six months he had escaped again. In January 1978, he attacked four women in the Chi Omega sorority house at Florida State University in Tallahassee. Two of the women were killed and two were left seriously injured. An hour and a half later, he attacked another

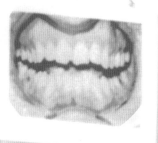

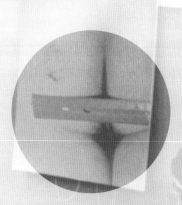

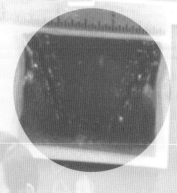

woman on the same campus. She survived and was able to provide a description.

Bundy was eventually recaptured in Pensacola and put on trial for the Florida murders. The crucial evidence was a bite mark on one of the victims that had been photographed and measured as part of the autopsy. Bundy's teeth were photographed and he was also forced to cooperate in the making of a cast of his bite. Because of peculiarities in the arrangement of his teeth in the jaw, which matched the injuries exactly, the jury accepted that he was the murderer. Once he had been convicted of the murders of the Florida State University students and sentenced to death, he intimated that he could have been responsible for a total of between forty and fifty murders. He was finally executed in 1989.

ABOVE Photographs of Bundy's teeth, which were linked to the bite-mark left on the buttock of one of the victims, Lisa Levy.

BACKGROUND Dr. Lowell Levine, chief consultant in forensic dentistry to the New York City Medical examiner, explaining the individual features of Bundy's teeth to the assembled court.

BELOW Dentist Dr. Richard Souviron shows the jury the bitemark evidence.

Trace Elements

ABOVE Highlighted spots of trace evidence on the road where murder victim James Byrd was dragged in Texas in 1998.

O ne of the basic assumptions of forensic science is that a person present at the scene of a crime exchanges trace evidence with the location in a number of different ways. Traces may be found at the scene that can be linked to a suspect, and traces found on the suspect may link him or her to the place where the crime was committed—or indeed to the crime itself. Hairs, fibers, particles of dust or soil, plant debris, paint flakes and other microscopic evidence can trap even scrupulously careful criminals and prove their involvement in the most meticulously planned crimes.

ABOVE Examining evidence through an optical microscope.

Paint Samples

Traces of paint evidence offer similar possibilities. In some cases the shape and color of a flake of paint can be matched with the surface from which it was taken. In others, the chemical constituents and other precise properties of the sample must be determined to prove whether or not they match the suspected source.

Paint samples are particularly important in cases involving vehicles, and forensic laboratories maintain large databases on the precise compositions and ranges of colors used by the larger manufacturers. The surface finish of any vehicle is usually built up as a series of layers, from the initial primer to the final coats of clear gloss. Colors can be compared under the microscope, and the polymer binder that holds each layer together can be broken down and analyzed by pyrolysis gas chromatography, where the paint chips are heated to release their constituents in gaseous form. This effectively creates a single "fingerprint" for each layer and helps to establish points of comparison with other samples.

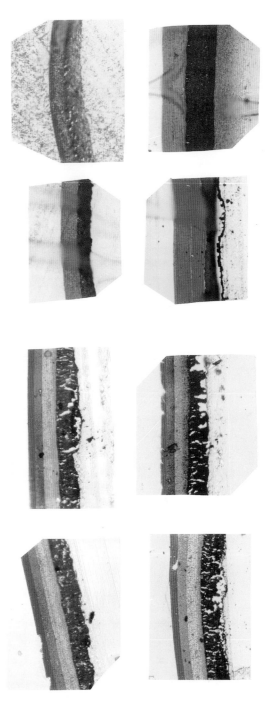

TOP FOUR Cross sections of different samples of red paint and underlying layers from different red automobiles.

BOTTOM FOUR Cross sections of red household paint.

TOP LEFT Kenneth Erskine, who was traced to a crime scene through samples of his hair.

Hairs

Hairs found at the scene may belong to the criminal, to the victim or to animals associated with either individual. Whatever their origin, hairs provide useful evidence because they retain their structure for a long time: the tough outer covering of the cuticle partly accounts for this resistance to decay. It is made from overlapping cells that show different patterns in different species of animal.

Inside the cuticle is the cortex, a regular array of cells running along the length of the hair. This carries the particles of pigment which give the hair its characteristic color. The way in which these particles are shaped and distributed, and their precise color, can help identify the hairs of particular individuals.

At the center of the cortex there is usually, but not always, another inner layer of cells called the medulla. The medulla is rarely continuous. In both human and animal hair, it may be interrupted or fragmented, and it varies in shape and appearance.

Unfortunately for investigators, there are often significant variations in the structure of different hairs from a single individual, especially if they are from different parts of the body. For this reason the widest possible range of comparison samples is taken for analysis. In general, hairs from the head are of circular cross-section, as are those from eyebrows and eyelashes, though these generally have more tapering tips. Hairs from the beard are generally triangular in cross section, while those from the armpits are oval.

Racial differences can sometimes be discerned by examination of the hair alone. People of Mongoloid origin, for example, tend to have hairs with a continuous medulla, while the particles of pigment in Afro-Caribbean hair are denser and less evenly distributed than those in Caucasian hair.

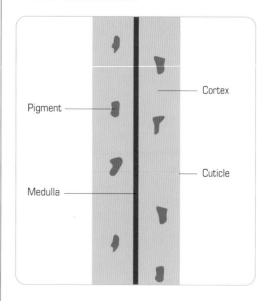

ABOVE Diagram showing the different internal components of a human hair.

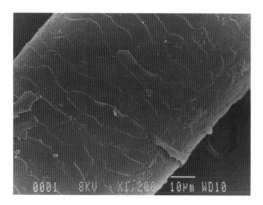

ABOVE Photomicrograph of a human hair, magnified 1200 times.

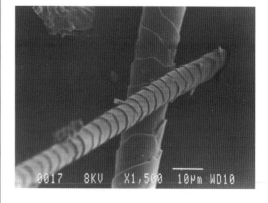

ABOVE Photomicrograph of a cat hair to the same scale as the human hair (left) is clearly thinner, with a different pattern of overlapping scales.

Using microscope technology, it is possible to tell whether a hair has been artificially bleached or colored. Depending on where the colored or bleached zone ends relative to the root of the hair, estimates can be made of when the last coloring or bleaching was actually applied.

Hairs can sometimes reveal the presence of poison in the body of the person they came from. In cases of drug abuse or poisoning by arsenic, the part of the hair in which these traces are found gives an indication of when doses were administered.

Further information can be gathered through neutron activation analysis, a process that was introduced in the late 1950s. A sample of potential evidence, such as a hair, is bombarded with neutrons in the core of a nuclear reactor. The neutrons collide with the atoms of the different trace elements making up the sample and render them radioactive. By measuring the resulting gamma radiation, the most minute traces of every constituent of the sample can be measured. Neutron activation analysis can identify traces of billionths of grams of fourteen different elements in a single hair. Calculations have shown that the likelihood of two different individuals having the same concentrations of just nine of these constituents is around one in a million. More recently, this powerful but fairly cumbersome

ABOVE Preparing a hair sample for microscopic analysis.

technique has been superseded by the use of hair as a source for producing samples of a subject's DNA (see Chapter Fourteen).

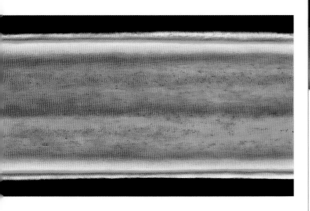

ABOVE Photograph of a human hair taken under polarized light, revealing the medulla as a darker central filament.

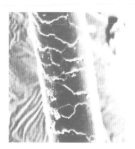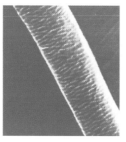

Fibers

All fibers used in clothing and furnishing fabrics are natural, man-made, or a combination of the two. Natural fibers include wool and silk, vegetable fibers like cotton, hemp, sisal, flax (used in making linen) and jute; a wide range of animal hairs such as cashmere, camel hair, mohair and alpaca; and furs like mink or sable. Each one has a characteristic appearance that enables it to be

ABOVE, FROM LEFT TO RIGHT Dog, deer, rabbit and horse hair.

BELOW False-color scanning electron micrograph of cotton fibers and (bottom) sheep hairs, one broken to show its internal honeycomb structure.

distinguished from human and other animal hairs when examined under a microscope.

As with most fiber evidence, the usefulness of any particular sample depends on its rarity. Cotton, for example, is so widely used in clothing that the presence of undyed cotton fibers is normally of little use, though different dyed colors can narrow the field to a significant extent. Animal hairs found at a crime scene may belong to pets rather than furs, and these too need to be checked carefully with any traces found on a suspect's clothing.

Man-made fibers, however, offer much more to the forensic examiner. Since the development of rayon and nylon before World War Two, a wide range of different materials has been produced including acetates, acrylics, and polyesters, each of which has different properties and identifiable characteristics. They are all formed from polymers, molecules built up from long chains containing millions of individual atoms that account for the elasticity and durability of many of these fabrics.

It is sometimes possible to identify fragments of fabric without sophisticated technology. For example, forensic examiners can sometimes match a length of fabric from the clothing of a hit-and-run victim with a fragment found on the vehicle responsible

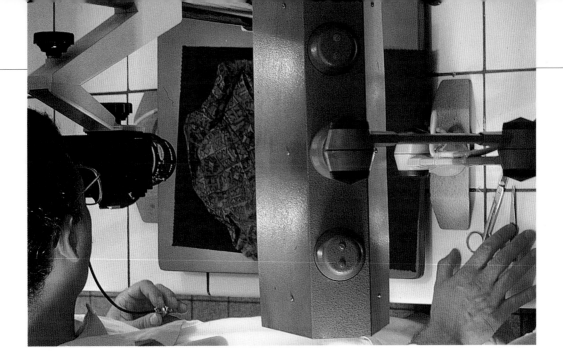

without needing to ascertain precise details of the material's composition.

More often, however, forensic examiners find relatively few fibers, so their value as evidence depends on their exact constitution. This can be checked through a microscope by pinpointing the fiber's precise diameter, its exact color, and any other distinguishing features such as striations running along the fibers from the production process, or particles of agents such as titanium dioxide, which is added during manufacture to modify the fabric's texture and surface shine.

The colors of fibers, even when only small fragments have been retrieved, can be compared very accurately by a technique

ABOVE Detailed forensic analysis of clothing taken from a crime scene.

called microspectrophotometry. This involves shining a beam of visible or infrared light on a sample of the fiber under a microscope to display the absorption spectrum of the fiber on a computer screen.

Chromatography can be used to separate the individual chemicals used to make the dye by dissolving the dye in a suitable solution. The fiber itself can be identified by additional tests such as birefringence. This is carried out by shining a beam of light onto a synthetic fiber: the light emerges refracted and polarized. The light emerging parallel to the axis of the fiber has one refractive index; that emerging perpendicular to the axis has another. By measuring the two refractive indices accurately, the fiber type can be identified.

BELOW, LEFT TO RIGHT Synthetic fibers, showing discernible differences in structure: acetate, nylon, and vivrelle.

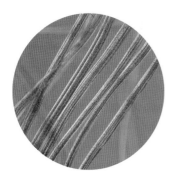

Glass and Dust Analysis

Samples of glass from vehicle windows or headlights, or from windows or glassware at the crime scene, can provide important evidence. Large fragments of glass can sometimes be fitted into the lamp or window pane from which they were broken for a positive match, or the glass can actually preserve a record of the order in which events happened. When a window pane is penetrated by a series of gunshots, for example, the first shot makes a hole surrounded by a set of radial fractures that in turn are linked by concentric fractures. These fracture patterns can tell forensic examiners which side of the glass received the initial blow from the stress marks along their cross section. Because developing fractures stop at the point of any existing fracture lines, the radial fractures from a second bullet hole end where they meet the radial fractures from the first. Fractures produced by a third bullet hole terminate where they meet fractures radiating from the first two, and so on.

Different types of glass have different densities and refractive indices. Density is measured by placing the glass fragments in a mixture of two chemicals of different known densities: bromoform and bromobenzene. The proportions of the two ingredients are adjusted until the glass particles remain suspended in the liquid, at which point their densities are equal.

The refractive index of glass is determined by immersing samples in a liquid that changes its refractive index according to its temperature. Controlled heat is applied until the contrast between the liquid and the glass particles disappears, at which point the refractive indices of the glass and the liquid are the same.

Although a particular combination of density and refractive index is not usually unique, the FBI laboratory maintains data on the frequency with which any individual combination is likely to be found. If two samples with the same properties come from a relatively rare type of glass, their significance in terms of evidence is increased.

Particles of dust picked up at the crime scene or on a suspect's clothing can also reveal important evidence. Soil from gardens, open land, tracks or woodland can be valuable because of the plant spores, pollen particles, insects and micro-organisms contained in it, all of which can be revealed by microscopic analysis and can help to indicate its likely source. Other dust particles of concrete, flour, coal or brick, for example, can suggest connections with a person's place of work or occupation.

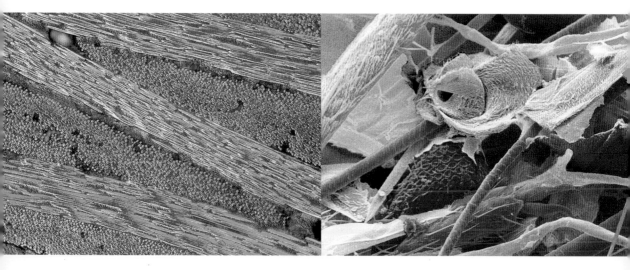

ABOVE Bullet holes in a glass window producing radial and concentric fractures, where the intersections reveal the order in which the shots struck the glass.

FAR LEFT Photomicrograph of glass fibers in a polypropylene matrix.

CENTER LEFT Color-scanning electron microscope image of household dust, made up of particles of soil and sand, skin scales, household fibers, and pet hair.

LEFT False-color scanning electron micrograph of glass fibers.

Stephen Bradley

ABOVE Confident kidnapper Stephen Bradley, trapped by trace evidence.

On July 7, 1960, eight-year-old Graeme Thorne was snatched by a kidnapper while on his way home from school in Sydney, Australia. His parents, Bazil and Frieda Thorne, had won the state lottery five weeks previously, and their newfound wealth had clearly made them a target. Sure enough, the kidnapper made two telephone calls demanding a $52,500 ransom for the boy's safe return; then all communications ceased.

Witnesses claimed to have seen a blue 1955 Ford Customline in the vicinity on the day of the kidnapping. The boy's schoolbag was found, then his cap, coat and books. Finally, on August 16, his body was discovered ten miles from his home, wrapped in a rug. The boy had been suffocated and then clubbed to death. The evidence was taken to the Sydney forensic laboratory to be studied in detail.

Scientists found a curious pink granular substance on parts of the boy's clothing, together with animal and human hairs. There were also traces of mold on his shoes and socks. Analysis revealed that the animal hairs were almost certainly from a Pekinese dog and that the pink grains came from a mortar used in house-building. The development of the mold indicated that the boy had probably been dead for five to six weeks, and so had been killed almost immediately after the kidnapping. Investigators also set out to identify all the plant material found on the rug and the body. Their finds included seeds of a rare variety of cypress that did not grow in the area where the body was discovered. A public appeal asked for details of houses that had both pink mortar between the bricks and this type of cypress in the garden. One such house was located in the suburb of Clontarf, where the tenants gave promising details of the previous occupant. He had been a Hungarian and had assumed the name of Stephen Bradley. His spoken English had been heavily accented—much like that of the man who had made the ransom demands—and he had left the house on the day of the kidnapping. A search of the premises yielded a picture of

OPPOSITE A handcuffed Bradley arrives at Sydney Coroner's Court.

Bradley, picnicking with his family on the very rug that had been used to wrap the boy's body. A tassel that had become detached from the rug was also found in the house.

Bradley was also known to have had a Pekinese dog, and to have sold a blue Ford Customline on the day of his disappearance. Police located the car at a local dealer's and found traces of pink mortar in the trunk. The dog, whose hairs matched those found on the boy's clothes, was traced to a veterinary hospital. Bradley himself was found, bound for England on the liner *Himalaya*. The ship was intercepted at Colombo in Sri Lanka, and Bradley was arrested. At trial he was convicted of the boy's murder and sentenced to life imprisonment.

Malcolm Fairley

ABOVE Multiple rapist Malcolm Fairley, alias "The Fox."

A series of burglaries and attacks on householders in southern England in 1984 became increasingly serious when the attacks began to escalate into violent assaults. The burglar threatened his victims with a shotgun he had stolen from one of his earlier robberies, and eventually took to raping his female victims and assaulting their male companions.

The man wore a hooded mask, but witnesses were able to report that he spoke with a northern-England accent and was clearly left-handed. Though a huge police hunt was mounted for the man, dubbed "The Fox" by newspaper reporters, he managed to evade capture for months.

On the night of August 17, however, when driving north to Yorkshire to visit his mother, "The Fox" made a careless mistake. He stopped on the outskirts of a village called Brampton and decided to strike again, even though he had left his hood at home. He concealed his car in a field and cut a new mask from a pair of green overalls. He then walked to the village, broke into a house, tied up the male occupant and raped his wife. He then coolly removed traces of physical evidence, even cutting away a square of bed sheet, and left.

When police searched the area they found tracks that showed where the car had been parked. They also found a flake of yellow paint where the car had scraped against a tree while being reversed into the hiding place, a leather glove, the piece of bed sheet and the burglar's crudely-made mask. Nearby, under a covering of leaves, they found the shotgun. Convinced that the suspect would return to retrieve the gun, police mounted a stake-

RIGHT Detective Chief Inspector John Branscombe shows the crudely made hood worn by "The Fox" during his attacks, against a background of other pieces of evidence, including gloves, shotgun cartridges, and a sawed-off shotgun.

RIGHT Armed police officers at Linslade Wood, near Leighton Buzzard, searching for the rapist known as "The Fox."

BELOW The search for "The Fox" extends to a house in the Bedfordshire village of Edlesborough.

out operation, staging a fake road accident to account for their presence in this quiet country area; but the suspect did not return.

The paint sample was analyzed and the color identified as "Harvest Gold." That color had been used on only one model, an Austin Allegro made between May 1973 and August 1975. Police also searched the national computer for details of burglars from the north of England who were known to have moved south, and the computer produced data on more than 3000 potential suspects.

The laborious police search continued until September 11, when two officers went to check an address in north London. The resident was one Malcolm Fairley, and officers found him outside washing his car—an Austin Allegro, painted in Harvest Gold. They questioned him about his recent movements, noting the pronounced northern accent that characterized his evasive answers. On the back seat of the car was the suspect's watch, which the police asked him to put on. He complied, and in doing so showed he was left-handed. The car itself bore evidence of damage at a height consistent with position of the paint flake found on the tree near Brampton. Fairley's flat was subsequently searched and two more sets of overalls identical to those used to make the mask were discovered. The suspect confessed and on February 26, 1985, Macolm Fairley was given six life sentences for a series of violent attacks and rapes.

BACKGROUND Malcolm Fairley's apartment in Kentish Town, North London.

John Vollman

On a spring afternoon in May 1958, sixteen-year-old Gaetane Bouchard failed to return from a shopping trip in Edmundston, New Brunswick, Canada. Her anxious father telephoned her friends to ask if they knew where she might be. Several mentioned a boyfriend, a twenty-year-old printer and part-time musician named John Vollman who lived across the U.S. border in Madawaska, Maine. When asked about Gaetane, Vollman claimed he had not seen her since he had become engaged to another woman.

Bouchard notified the police and resumed his search. He checked an abandoned gravel pit that was popular with young couples in parked cars—and there he found his daughter's body. She had been stabbed to death. At the scene police found tire tracks, and two flakes of green paint that had probably been dislodged from a vehicle by stones thrown up by its wheels as it accelerated away.

Witnesses were found who reported that, earlier that day, Gaetane had been seen buying chocolate. She had also been seen talking to the driver of a 1952 green Pontiac with Maine license plates, and been seen inside the car, which was thought to be the vehicle that had left tracks at the murder scene.

Detectives checked Vollman's car and were able to match the larger paint flake with a corresponding chipped patch below the passenger door. Inside the glove compartment there was also a half-eaten bar of chocolate bearing traces of lipstick. The most important evidence, however, was a hair found clutched in the dead girl's hand.

Samples of Gaetane's hair, Vollman's hair and the hair found at the scene were tested by neutron activation analysis (see page 177). One result gave the ratio of sulfur radiation to phosphorus radiation in each sample: Gaetane's hair registered 2.02, Vollman's registered 1.07 and the sample found clasped in her hand registered 1.02.

Though Vollman's attorneys attempted to have the evidence rejected as inadmissible, it prompted Vollman to change his plea of innocence to one of guilty of manslaughter. Nevertheless he was convicted of murder and sentenced to death (the sentence was later commuted to life imprisonment) and he became the first criminal to be convicted by the powerful new technique of neutron activation analysis.

ABOVE Scanning electron micrograph of the surface of a shaft of human hair shows how irregular each individual strand can be.

Blood

ABOVE Murder victim Ghislaine Marchal apparently wrote the words "Omar killed me" in her own blood on the door of the room where she died, and the message provided vital evidence in the conviction of her accused attacker, Omar Raddad.

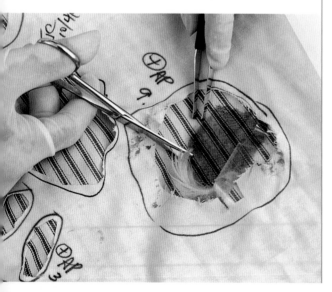

An adult has some ten pints of blood circulating around the body, driven under pressure from the heart's pumping action. This presents a potential attacker with something of a problem. Any cutting or piercing of major blood vessels can produce a deluge and result in significant traces of blood being left at a crime scene. Such traces can indicate how an attack was made and help identify all manner of objects associated with it. Even the attacker's own blood, shed in a violent struggle, can tie him or her to the scene as securely as a photograph or an eyewitness identification.

LEFT Checking bloodstains on a pillow recovered from a crime scene.

For these reasons, criminals often go to great lengths to remove bloodstains from a crime scene. They may satisfy themselves that all traces have been eliminated, but once the crime has been discovered the police search usually extends to areas beyond the perpetrators' control. Forensic experts check beneath washbasins and inside drawers, between floorboards or in drains and waste-pipes leading from baths or sinks that may have been used for washing or for cleaning the murder weapon.

Bloodstain evidence

At one time, blood found at the crime scene was significant to forensic scientists simply by its presence. Because blood tends to dry quickly on exposure to air and to remain clearly visible unless cleaned away, bloodstains and splashes can often tell their own story. Drops of blood that fall onto a horizontal surface, for example, give examiners some idea of how far they fell before hitting the surface,

and so suggest the position at the time of the individual who shed the blood.

If the blood falls only a short distance, the marks are circular or, if the surface is at an

ABOVE Bloody footprints provide evidence at a crime scene.

BELOW At the crime scene collecting blood samples for analysis.

angle to the horizontal, elliptical in shape. If the drops fall a few feet before hitting the surface, the edges of the circular mark are crenellated, the degree of crenellation increasing proportionately with the length of the fall. If drops fall from a height of six feet or so, there are usually side spurts radiating from the site of the main drop.

Drops of blood shed from a moving source have a different appearance. They may have fallen from an already blood-soaked weapon being swung to deliver a blow, or from a wounded victim trying to escape. In such cases any drops hitting floors or walls often take on the appearance of a stretched exclamation mark: the end of the stain showing the smaller blob indicates the direction of the subject's movement.

Stains made by blood spurting under pressure from a major blood vessel show where a serious or even fatal blow was delivered. The height reached by the spurting blood, if it splashed on a wall or partition, for example, can show whether the victim was standing, sitting, kneeling or lying down when the blow was struck; the quantity of blood spilled, when compared with injuries to the victim's body, can be correlated with particular wounds. Pools of blood can also indicate where the victim died, even if the body was later moved.

Tests for blood

In many cases, blood spilled at a crime scene is all too obvious. But even if criminals have tried to clean away the evidence, examiners must ensure that they locate every remaining trace. There are several chemicals that can differentiate between blood and other substances with a similar appearance, and others that can be used to highlight bloodstains. In using these chemicals at the scene, great care must be taken to avoid contamination, since some of the tests are sensitive to chemicals other than blood. The first test simply uses a powerful light. The

ABOVE Portable blood test kit for field and laboratory use.

BELOW Forensic scientist places a sample of bloodstained clothing into a sample tube for analysis.

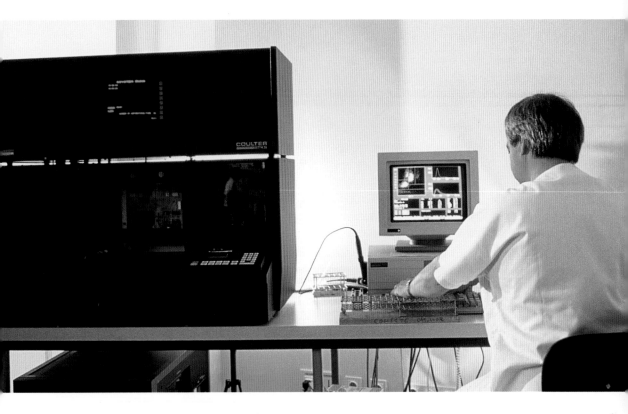

light's beam, held at an angle over every surface at the scene, can often reveal traces of blood that would otherwise remain unnoticed.

A more powerful test relies on a chemical called luminol, which reacts with blood to produce a faint luminescence. Examiners darken the room being tested and spray all suspect areas with the chemical. All spots and stains of blood then emit a faint blue glow, the intensity of which varies according to the amount of blood present. The test works even on old bloodstains, which react by glowing more vividly than recent marks. Luminol can reveal bloodstains even if they are diluted by a factor of 10,000, but it does have one unfortunate drawback. The chemical can destroy many of the properties of bloodstains that examiners need to preserve for further analysis, so it is normally used only to check for bloodstains that would otherwise remain invisible to the naked eye.

If examiners wish to confirm that suspicious-looking marks are in fact bloodstains, chemical indicators such as phenolphthalein can be used. When mixed with hydrogen peroxide and a blood sample, these chemicals react with the hemoglobin in the red cells to produce a deep pink color. Unfortunately, they also react in a similar way to constituents of potatoes and horseradish, so examiners must guard against any potential contamination from such sources.

To identify blood as human blood, a sample is placed in a test tube above a layer of specially prepared rabbit serum that has been sensitized to human blood. This is prepared by injecting a rabbit with human blood, allowing the appropriate antibodies to form in the animal's bloodstream, then extracting a sample. If the sample found at the crime scene is human blood, a cloudy ring will appear at the junction of the suspect sample and the rabbit serum.

Blood groups

Blood is a mixture of red and white blood cells suspended in a watery liquid called plasma. Plasma accounts for more than half the blood's content. The job of the red blood cells is to absorb oxygen from the lungs and carry it to the body tissues. The red cells carry chemicals called antigens that can react to the presence of blood of a different group by causing the cells to clump together, or agglutinate. This adverse reaction caused the death of many patients given blood in early transfusions toward the end of the nineteenth century.

In 1901, Austrian biologist Dr. Karl Landsteiner identified two different blood groups, A and B, that had different antigens on their red cells. He found that blood of either type could be mixed with blood of the same type from a different person without any adverse reaction, but if the two types were mixed with each other, agglutination occurred. Landsteiner subsequently identified a third group that he classified as type C, and this had affinities with both type A and type B. A fourth

group was also found that could be mixed with groups A or B without agglutination, and this was classified as group AB.

In time further human blood classifications were defined and the Rhesus factor recognized. The Rhesus is an antigen occurring in the red cells of most people: where it is present, the blood is described as Rhesus positive (Rh+); where it is not, the blood is described as Rhesus negative (Rh-). Different enzymes and proteins were also isolated, and these can now be identified even in dried bloodstains, adding further detail to investigators' findings.

Every detail extracted from a blood sample helps to narrow the field of possible sources. For example, some forty-two percent of the U.S. population has type A blood, about nine percent has type B, forty-six percent type O and three percent type AB. An enzyme called phosphoglucomutase 2-1 (PGM2-1) is also found in thirty-six percent of the population, regardless of blood group. So if PGM2-1 is found in a sample of type A blood, for example, the field of potential sources is narrowed to 0.36 x 0.42 or fifteen percent of the population. Traces or absences of other proteins and enzymes can be used to identify an individual blood sample more particularly, with the result in some cases that the field of possible sources is narrowed to hundredths of one percent of the population. Such accuracy is of course highly useful in both eliminating or implicating suspects.

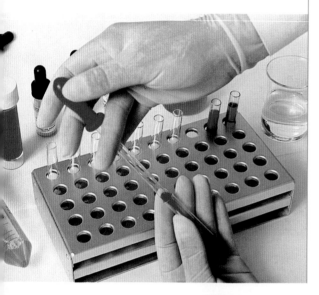

TOP LEFT A gloved hand transferring blood into a sample bottle.

LEFT AND ABOVE Blood from a shoe is reconstituted in a saline solution before being dropped into a test tube (above) containing different antibodies to determine the blood group.

RIGHT A program called FAScan displays the results of blood analysis.

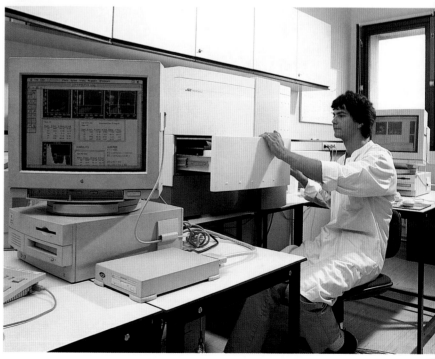

Secretors

Irrespective of blood group, around eighty percent of the population qualify as "secretors" because the antigens, antibodies, proteins and enzymes that characterize their blood are also found in other body fluids like tears, sweat, saliva, vaginal fluids and semen. The remaining twenty percent or so of the population carry this information only in the blood; but in secretors, samples of skin and muscle tissue, and even saliva left by a smoker on the butt of a cigarette can contain a great deal of evidence. Forensic examination is then simplified by the fact that just a sample of saliva, which can be quickly and easily obtained once a suspect is identified, can be tested and the results checked against crime-scene evidence.

ABOVE Two pieces of bloodstained cloth and a vaginal swab from a rape investigation.

BELOW A forensic serology laboratory, specializing in testing and analysis of body fluids.

RIGHT Photomicrograph of human spermatozoa.

Seminal fluid

In cases of rape and other sexual crimes, the seminal fluid left by the attacker on the victim's body or on clothing or furniture presents another powerful source of evidence. Since the sperm in the fluid remain alive for only a relatively short period, the condition of the sample can give a reasonably accurate indication of the time of the attack. In the case of secretors, such a sample contains information on blood group and the presence or absence of other enzymes and proteins that can help to concentrate the search for a potential subject.

Samples of seminal fluid are isolated using tests similar to those used to reveal the presence of bloodstains. These tests are particularly useful where attempts have been made by the criminal to remove or wash away incriminating traces.

The usual test is for the presence of an enzyme called acid phosphatase, which is normally secreted into the seminal fluid by the prostate gland. Filter paper is rubbed over the suspected area and any acid phosphatase present is partly transferred to the paper. A few drops of a mixture of sodium alphanaphthylphosphate and a chemical called Fast Blue B solution are then dropped on the paper, and if the enzyme is present a deep purple color quickly appears. Again, the test is sensitive to other substances such as fungi and some types of fruit and vegetable juice, but these fluids do not usually produce a reaction as quickly as seminal fluid does.

Another more specific test developed in the 1970s looks for a protein called p30 or Prostate Specific Antigen (PSA). This is found only in seminal fluid and the test is similar in principle to that used to identify bloodstains as human. A sample of p30 is injected into a rabbit to induce the animal to produce antibodies to the protein. Then a sample of blood serum containing this antibody (anti-p30) is taken from the rabbit and used to test the

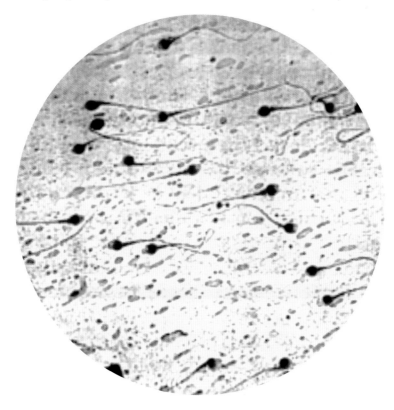

ABOVE FROM LEFT TO RIGHT Suspect semen extract and sample of anti-p30 added to their respective wells of an electrophoretic plate; antigen and antibody move towards one another under electric charge; formation of a visible straight line between the two wells reveals the suspect fluid contains semen.

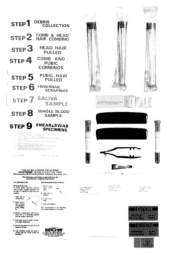

STEP 1 DEBRIS COLLECTION
STEP 2 COMB & HEAD HAIR COMBING
STEP 3 HEAD HAIR PULLED
STEP 4 COMB AND PUBIC COMBINGS
STEP 5 PUBIC HAIR PULLED
STEP 6 FINGERNAIL SCRAPINGS
STEP 7 SALIVA SAMPLE
STEP 8 WHOLE BLOOD SAMPLE
STEP 9 SMEAR&SWAB SPECIMENS

ABOVE Sex crimes investigation kit used by England's Metropolitan Police.

LEFT Array of blood samples being analyzed for DNA fingerprinting.

OPPOSITE PAGE Forensic scientist removes bloodstained material from clothing for DNA fingerprinting.

suspect sample for seminal fluid. The suspect trace is placed in one well of an electrophoretic plate, and the anti-p30 rabbit serum in the other. When an electric charge is applied across the plate, if the antibodies and antigens start to move toward one another and eventually form a visible straight line between the two wells, then the sample is seminal fluid.

More recently, these complex tests for different blood groups and the presence of different proteins and enzymes have been

overtaken by the much more powerful technique of retrieving DNA from victims and suspects (see Chapter Fourteen). The DNA test produces an accurate and entirely individual result that can convict a criminal on the basis of the smallest trace of bodily fluid, quite independently of other corroborative evidence. As this technique becomes better known, of course, criminals are responding by adapting their methods of operation and leaving as few personal traces as possible.

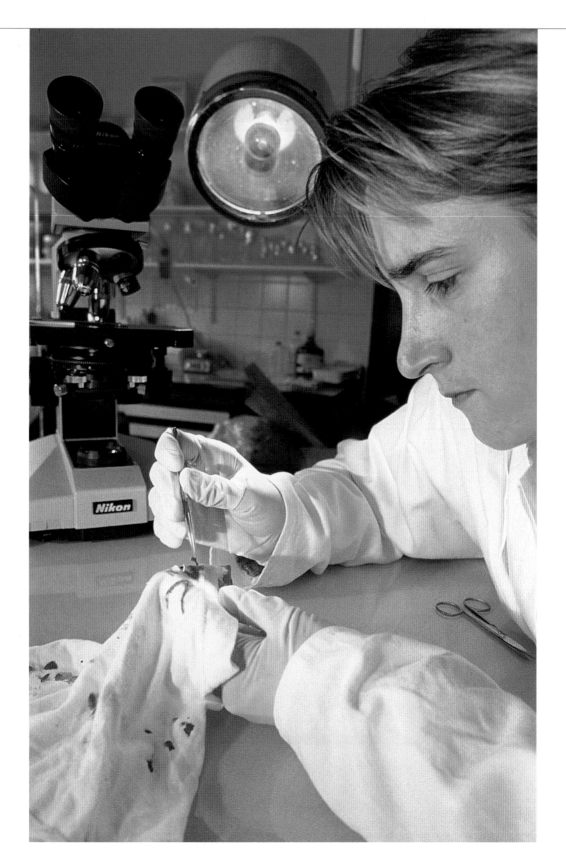

Lindy Chamberlain

Michael and Lindy Chamberlain took their two sons, aged six and four, and their nine-week-old daughter Azaria on a camping holiday to the interior of Australia in August 1980. The family pitched their tent at a site close to the huge and mysterious landmark of Uluru (Ayers Rock). The following day Michael climbed to the top of the rock twice, taking his young sons with him on the second climb.

On the evening of August 17, the baby was snugly cocooned in blankets in a baby carrier at the back of the tent where the younger boy was also asleep. Lindy Chamberlain was cooking supper for the older boy at the barbecue site some sixty feet away: the tent flap was left unzipped since the boy would be going to bed after his meal. Michael Chamberlain claimed he heard a short, sharp cry at around eight o'clock, and Lindy started back to the tent to check the baby.

Lindy Chamberlain later told of her astonishment at this point when she saw an Australian wild dog, or dingo, backing out of the tent and shaking something violently in its jaws. The dingo disappeared into the darkness, whereupon the horrified Chamberlains found their baby was missing. The alarm was raised and trackers mounted a search of the surrounding countryside, but no sign of the baby or the dingo was found.

To the surprise of many onlookers, the deeply religious couple seemed to accept their daughter's disappearance quite calmly, and to assume that she would not be found alive. Suspicions mounted when, eight days after the baby's disappearance, most of her clothes were found by a tourist walking through scrub to the west of Ayers Rock. The clothes were neatly folded, but the jacket was missing. The undershirt was inside out; the bootees were still laced up and were found inside the legs of the baby's jumpsuit. There were bloodstains around the neck of the jumpsuit and on the undershirt, but there were no signs of any human remains in the clothes or at the scene.

When the clothes were examined in detail, other curious facts emerged. There were no traces of dingo hair or dingo saliva on the garments, even in the area of the bloodstains. Controversial experiments were carried out in which dead animals of a size similar to that of the baby and clad in similar clothes were thrown into the dingo pen at Adelaide Zoo. The dogs' responses were observed and recorded. Investigators concluded that, since there were no pulled threads on Azaria's clothing or any other indications of a dingo being involved, the child must have been attacked by humans who had subsequently removed her clothes and left them several miles from the camp site.

BACKGROUND Lindy Chamberlain and her husband Michael, a pastor with the Seventh Day Adventist Church, entering the court at Alice Springs in 1982.

Tests on the garment bloodstains showed that the blood could have come from a child of parents with the Chamberlains' blood groups. The bloodstains also showed that the undershirt had been worn the right way round when the staining occurred and had then been turned inside out. It was also apparent that the top two studs of the jumpsuit had been unfastened, though they had been fastened when the bleeding took place. The pattern of the bloodstains suggested that the child's injuries had been inflicted by a cut to the throat with a knife rather than by any kind of animal bite. It was also reported that two bloodstained prints of small adult hands were found on the jumpsuit.

ABOVE Michael and Lindy Chamberlain with their attorney.

Suspicion began to center on the Chamberlains themselves. Stains of blood from a child less than six months old were found in their car: on the carpet, around the supports for the front seats and on the blade, handle and hinges of a pair of scissors in the vehicle. The couple were tried in September 1982 for the murder of their baby daughter, and though both partners pleaded not guilty, in October Lindy was convicted of the murder and Michael Chamberlain was convicted as an accessory.

The trial attracted continuing controversy, and much of the prosecution evidence came under attack. The "handprints," for example, were said to be random bloodstains; it was also difficult to see when and where the Chamberlains would have had the opportunity to kill the baby and dispose of the body on a packed campsite. Two appeals were mounted, but they were unsuccessful and Lindy Chamberlain remained in prison.

In 1986, controversy resurfaced with the discovery of the baby's missing jacket, now torn and bloodstained, in a dingo cave near the campsite. In the light of this new evidence, Lindy Chamberlain was released. There was apparently a wealth of evidence in this case, but too much of it was open to more than one interpretation, and ultimately too much remained unexplained to settle the important questions beyond reasonable doubt. In June 1987 the couple were officially pardoned, and in September 1988 their convictions were quashed.

RIGHT Lindy Chamberlain pictured in 1986 arriving at court in Darwin to attend the enquiry into her conviction.

DNA: the Ultimate Identifier?

ABOVE Laboratory culture dishes and glassware lying on top of a DNA profile.

From the earliest days of forensic science, those engaged in tracking down criminals of all kinds have longed for some universal identifier, some attribute entirely unique to each individual that would be difficult or impossible to disguise. At one time fingerprints seemed to offer the answer, until careful criminals learned to wear gloves, or to wipe prints off every surface they might have touched at the scene. At last, the answer has been found—and it lies in something more fundamental to the individual than superficial patterns on the fingertips: it lies in the cells.

Every human being is made up of vast numbers of living cells of different types. Inside the nucleus of every cell there is a string of coded information in the form of a ribbonlike molecule of deoxyribonucleic acid (DNA) that contains the genetic blueprint of that particular person's makeup. Because everyone's genetic make-up is unique, this coded information is as individual as a perfect set of fingerprints with the added advantage to forensic investigators that the information is almost impossible to eliminate.

Each DNA molecule is actually a polymer, or a long-chain molecule made up of repeated units called nucleotides. Each one of these nucleotides consists of a molecule of sugar bound to another containing phosphorus and another containing nitrogen. The complete DNA molecule contains millions of these nucleotides, arranged in pairs on two long chains or strands, curved into a spiral or helix within the cell nucleus.

The amount of information contained in these codes is prodigious. Each human cell contains a string of twenty-three pairs of chromosomes, each of which contains almost one hundred thousand genes and DNA chains made up of one hundred million base pairs. So the complete human genetic code involves some three billion base pairs, controlling everything from height and build to color of hair and eyes.

BELOW James Watson (left) and Francis Crick, discoverers of the structure of DNA, with their model of part of the DNA helix in 1953. They shared the Nobel Prize for physiology or medicine with Maurice Wilkins, who specialized in X-ray crystallography.

ABOVE Computer-generated image of the DNA double helix.

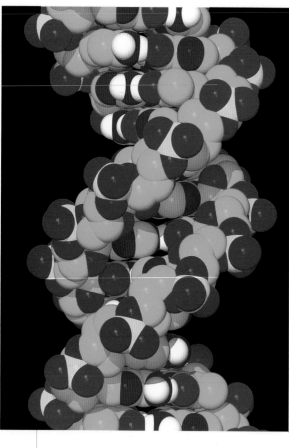

LEFT Computer graphic image of part of a DNA molecule with the atoms represented as colored spheres: yellow for phosphorus, red for oxygen, green for carbon, blue for nitrogen and white for hydrogen.

BELOW Nucleotides linking together to form the DNA strand, with S representing a sugar molecule, joined to a phosphate group to form the spine of the chain, and four bases (A for adenine, G for guanine, T for thymine and C for cytosine) that provide the links to the other half of the double helix.

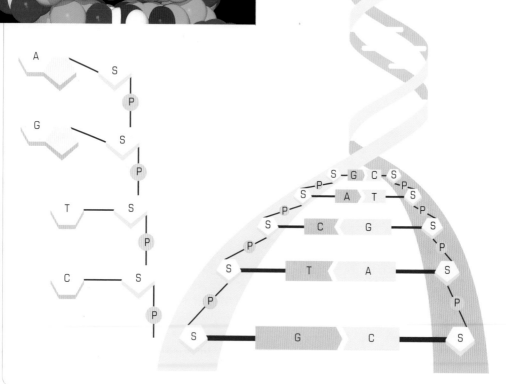

The DNA code

The DNA nucleotides are linked together to form the DNA chain with their sugar and phosphate molecules alternating. Each sugar molecule has one of four types of nitrogen compound molecules (or "bases") attached to it. These are adenine (A), cytosine (C), guanine (G) or thymine (T). The complete chain contains millions of these bases and uses these four basic building blocks in different combinations to draw up the blueprint for a complete living organism.

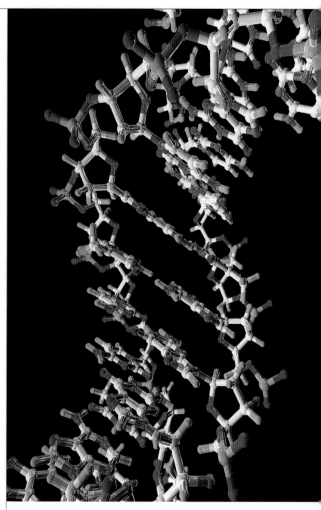

ABOVE Computer image of part of a DNA strand in all its complexity—in this case carbon is white, hydrogen pale blue, nitrogen is dark blue, oxygen red and phosphorus orange.

ABOVE Intertwined strands of DNA representing segments of two chromosomes—the one on the left has three repeating sequences of T, A and G bases, and the right-hand one has only two.

Inside each living cell, the double helix is formed by the bases of one DNA strand joining those of the other in specific combinations, rather like the rungs of an almost endless ladder. When the cell divides to form two new cells, the double helix splits into two single strands, each of which forms the nucleus of a new cell, combining with other nucleotides within the cell to form a new double helix identical to the original.

The DNA-coded sequence that specifies a single individual initially seemed to scientists to be an impossibly long and complex set of instructions. Yet it became clear that, since human beings share many basic characteristics, large stretches of the genetic code must be common to all individuals. The DNA elements that could actually single out an individual were those particular extracts responsible for specific details such as physical appearance, family traits and color of eyes or hair.

203

Genetic markers

Scientists realized that some form of marker was needed to allow these polymorphic pieces of an individual's DNA code to be isolated so that they could be recorded and eventually compared with corresponding information from other individuals or samples. By the 1980s, a team of genetics researchers at the Lister Institute of the University of Leicester in England, led by Dr. Alec Jeffreys, had isolated particular parts of the DNA code by taking cell nuclei from a sample and using a substance called a restriction enzyme to cut the DNA chain at particular points. The enzyme did this by recognizing a sequence in the code and cutting the chain at specific points to produce a series of fragments of different lengths. These were then sorted by a technique called gel electrophoresis, in which a high-voltage electric current was applied to the DNA fragments in a gel.

RIGHT A laboratory technician carrying out gel electrophoresis to sort and identify DNA fragments.

BELOW Dr. (now Sir) Alec Jeffreys working in his laboratory.

Gel electrophoresis causes the different DNA fragments to move through the gel at different rates. The shorter pieces move more quickly than the longer ones, effectively sorting the different fragments according to their length. The fragments are then transferred to a special nylon membrane in much the same way as an ink line might be transferred to a sheet of blotting paper.

Individual sequences are then identified according to the code they contain using a radioactive marker. This is a genetic probe carrying a code that automatically binds to the genetic material being looked for. For example, to identify DNA fragments that contain the code sequence A-G-T (for adenine, guanine and thymine bases), a radioactive marker with the sequence T-C-A (for thymine, cytosine and adenine) is used, since these two combinations automatically bind together.

Building the "genetic fingerprint"

The nylon sheet containing the DNA fragments is then placed on X-ray-sensitive film. A radioactive genetic marker will have bound to those fragments containing the code sequence being studied, and this affects the film at the points where they appear. The resulting plate, when developed, reveals the positions of the DNA fragments carrying the radioactive markers. They appear in a series of bars not unlike the bar codes used to identify different products at a supermarket check-out. Just as the arrangement of thick and thin bars and white spaces in a barcode identifies each different product, so samples of DNA show the coded sequences in arrangements unique to each individual, providing a genetic

BELOW Computer display from an automated method for decoding sequences of base-pairs in fragments of DNA extracted from the chromosomes in human cells—"DNA fingerprinting."

"fingerprint." The pattern on the "fingerprint" is different in every case, except where identical twins or other identical multiple births are involved.

In the future, this powerful technique will become faster and easier to use and the information it yields will be even more accurate. Existing methods of comparing the so-called "barcode" traces on an X-ray film are being replaced by a new technique developed by Dr. Jeffreys in 1991. This searches for short sequences of elements that are repeated within the DNA molecule. These sequences occur repeatedly throughout the DNA chain, and so can be retrieved from bodies or samples where the DNA has been degraded by decomposition or the passage of time, or from very small DNA samples that contain only incomplete material.

These sequences are isolated from the sample and amplified by a method called

BELOW DNA fingerprints used in paternity testing (top left) with prints of the mother's DNA shown in green, the child's in red and the potential father's in blue. Direct comparisons at the top right and bottom left show correspondence between all the bands in the child's DNA with either those of the mother or the true father, but the comparison with the DNA fingerprint of the alleged father at bottom right shows several mismatches, proving he could not be the father of the child.

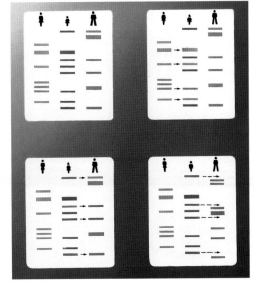

polymerase chain reaction (PCR) which can work with as little as a billionth of a gram of DNA material. The technique uses new knowledge about the way DNA replicates naturally in cell division and growth. PCR can magnify the amount of DNA originally extracted from the sample a million times in approximately an hour. The resulting DNA is then processed through gel electrophoresis to reveal the number of repeats of the basic sequence in each part of the sample.

Because there are hundreds of different types of these short sequences in human genes, a series of different searches extends into millions the odds against two individuals having the same DNA information. The information is now processed to yield a digital code of between fifty and seventy numbers. This precise record can be used to distinguish between DNAs from two or more sources found in the same sample, as they are sometimes in cases of rape or in the aftermath of a struggle. These digital records can also be stored in computer databases and transmitted virtually instantly across the world to be compared with others.

Rules of inheritance

Because each newborn child inherits half its chromosomes, together with their DNA, from each of its parents, any genetic fingerprint from the child's DNA must correspond in every detail with the equivalent genetic fingerprint of one parent or the other. The DNA of different offspring of the same couple have the

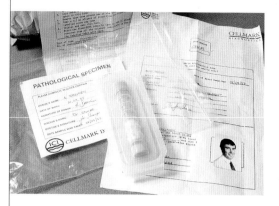

ABOVE A pathological specimen, bagged and waiting for analysis.

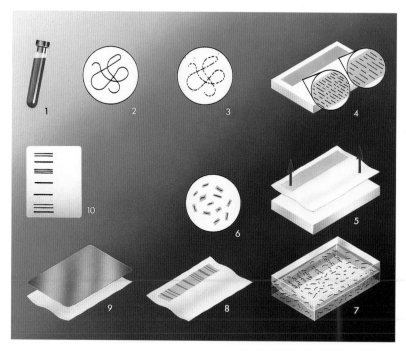

LEFT The DNA fingerprinting process—a blood sample (1) contains DNA (2) cut into fragments by a special enzyme (3) that are separated into bands of gel electrophoresis (4). A DNA band pattern is transferred to a nylon membrane (5) with a radioactive probe (6) which can recognize specific DNA sequences. The probe DNA binds to target DNA sequences on the nylon membrane (7) and excess DNA is washed off (8). An X-ray film is exposed to the radioactive DNA (9) and developed to reveal the characteristic bands that make up the DNA fingerprint (10).

same relationships with the parents' DNA. This creates the possibility of identifying individual DNA samples by reference to those of known relatives or descendants. It is even possible to reconstruct the DNA fingerprint of a missing parent from those of the remaining parent and their child.

This kind of investigation across the generations, or even the centuries, is made possible because of the extraordinary lasting qualities of DNA. Researchers have been able to extract DNA material from the bones of corpses burned long ago in an attempt to destroy their identity—and even from the mummified bodies of Egyptian pharaohs thousands of years old.

RIGHT Analysis and comparison of DNA fingerprints.

BELOW DNA testing used in anthropology research, to study family relationships and the transmission of hereditary diseases.

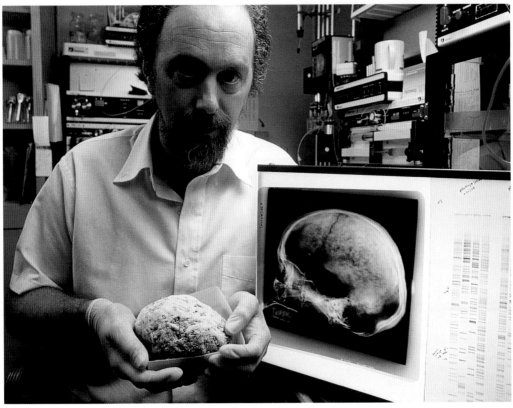

Colin Pitchfork

The rape and murder of fifteen-year-old schoolgirl Lynda Mann in the village of Narborough in Leicestershire in November 1983 horrified the local community. The only clue left by the killer was his semen which, even without DNA fingerprinting, proved to be of a type found in just ten percent of the adult male population. This at least allowed for the elimination of suspects, even if it could not be used for positive identification of the killer.

Because Lynda had been attacked and killed on a secluded footpath, police were confident that her murderer was a local man. Newspaper appeals for witnesses produced no helpful leads, however; nor did the police's door-to-door inquiries.

On July 31, 1986 another fifteen-year-old, Dawn Ashworth from Enderby, was raped and murdered on another quiet footpath, after having visited friends in Narborough. Soon afterward the police computer, searching for local people with records of sexual offences, identified a young kitchen porter at the Carlton Hayes mental hospital on the outskirts of the village. He was questioned by police and made a full confession, though this was later retracted. Nevertheless the police took a blood sample and asked Dr. Alec Jeffreys of Leicester University, the inventor of genetic fingerprinting, to compare the sample with that found on Lynda Mann's body.

The DNA evidence showed clearly that the kitchen porter was not responsible for either murder, but it also proved beyond all doubt that the same unknown man had killed both girls, and the police search was redoubled. With this precise DNA evidence on record, the police turned their attention back to the adult male population of Narborough and neighboring villages Littlethorpe and Enderby, only this time they were not just asking questions, they were asking for blood samples.

ABOVE Police collecting evidence at the scene of the murder of Lynda Mann.

BELOW Removing Lynda's body from the scene.

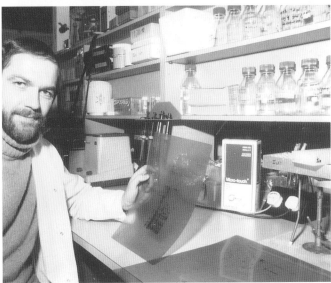

ABOVE Dawn Ashworth, the second murder victim.

RIGHT Dr. Alec Jeffreys analyzed the mass DNA samples in this case.

TOP RIGHT The pub where locals discussed Colin Pitchfork's payment to a fellow worker for giving a blood sample on his behalf.

In all, more than 4,500 men provided blood samples. According to the paperwork, one of these was Colin Pitchfork, a twenty-seven-year-old bakery worker who had been questioned earlier in the investigation. But on September 18, 1987, a policeman whose father was the owner of a local pub made an interesting report. Bakery workers had been heard discussing the fact that Colin Pitchfork had paid a workmate, Ian Kelly, to give a blood sample on his behalf. Police checked the signature at the blood test against Pitchfork's genuine signature, that appeared on the forms he signed during the original inquiry, and found the two did not match. Pitchfork was arrested and obliged to provide a blood sample: the sample confirmed that he was the double murderer. He confessed to the crime and in January 1988 was imprisoned for life.

ABOVE Colin Pitchfork.

Ian Simms

n the late afternoon of February 9, 1988, a twenty-two-year-old insurance clerk named Helen McCourt alighted from a bus and began the half-mile walk to her home in the village of Billinge in northwest England. She planned to stop on the way at the George and Dragon, the village pub, to see the owner, Ian Simms. Although Simms was married, he and McCourt had been having a relationship. He had tried to end the affair; nevertheless McCourt was intending to see him that evening.

After she got off the bus, Helen McCourt apparently vanished from the face of the earth. She did not return home and was never seen again, dead or alive.

Witnesses reported having heard a scream from the pub not long after McCourt left the bus, and police went to interview Ian Simms. There were scratches on Simms' face, which he told officers had been made during a fight with his wife. There was also soil trapped in the rings and a bracelet he was wearing, but he offered no explanation for that, nor could he account for the scream said to have been heard coming from his pub.

ABOVE Ian Simms.

RIGHT Local people join in the search for evidence after Helen McCourt's disappearance.

BELOW The jury outside the George and Dragon pub, where the murder took place.

Police took Simms' car for examination and found a bloodstained earring that had belonged to McCourt, together with long strands of hair. On searching Simms' rooms at the pub, they found a clip that matched the earring and patterns of bloodstains that suggested a fight had started inside the door, continued up the stairs and into a bedroom, and ended with the victim on the floor.

There were no signs of the woman's body, though one by one items that had belonged to her were retrieved from the countryside around the village. These included her purse, which was found with her coat and some other heavily bloodstained items of clothing. Hairs from Simms' two dogs were found on the coat, as were carpet fibers from his apartment, and the plastic bags in which the clothing was found were similar to those used at the pub. Also recovered was a knotted length of electrical cable that bore strands of hair matching those found in Simms' car. Both the hair samples were checked against samples of McCourt's hair taken from her bedroom at the family home, and both matched.

The remarkable feature of this case was the way in which DNA was used—in the absence of the victim's body—to prove that the blood in the apartment belonged to Helen McCourt. Blood samples were taken from both parents, and the DNA extracted from those samples was found to have very close similarities with the DNA extracted from the blood found at the George and Dragon. Using the parents' blood was one step away from using the blood of the victim herself, but Dr. Alec Jeffreys of the Lister Institute at the University of Leicester testified that the odds against any other sample providing as close a match were 14,500 to one. As a result, and in spite of the fact that Helen McCourt's body was never found, Simms was convicted of her murder and sentenced to life imprisonment.

BACKGROUND Helen McCourt, whose body was never found, but whose murderer was brought to justice through her parents' DNA.

Dr. Josef Mengele

ABOVE Dr Josef Mengele, taken in South America In 1960.

BELOW Wanted poster showing Mengele's photograph and an artist's impression of how he might have aged since the picture was taken.

A t the end of World War Two, one of the most notorious fugitives from justice was the chief medical officer at the Auschwitz death camp, Dr. Josef Mengele. He was responsible for the deaths of hundreds of thousands of the camp's inmates. Many of them, including young children, had died as a direct result of his barbarous experiments.

Rumors abounded as to his eventual fate, but the facts appeared to be that he had evaded capture in Germany for four years before fleeing to Argentina, where the trail had disappeared. In the mid-1980s, when international efforts were being made to track him down in his South American hideout, reports were received that Mengele was buried in a Brazilian village in a grave bearing the name Wolfgang Gerhard. The occupant of the grave, whatever his real identity, was listed as having drowned in 1979 at the age of sixty-seven.

The grave was opened and the body removed in June 1985, and all the techniques available were used to try to provide a positive identification. The problem was that the only known personal information about Mengele was contained in his S.S. personnel file. This was short on detail, giving only basic information such as Mengele's overall height and the circumference of his head. When forensic anthropologists examined the bones from the grave they found the occupant was Caucasian, from the shape of the eye socket and nose. The pelvic bones suggested the body had been male, and characteristics of the arm bones indicated he had been right-handed. Judging by the wear of the teeth, the man had been between sixty and seventy years old when he died.

At that time, the only further checks that could be made to try to establish the body's identity involved comparing X-rays of the teeth with Mengele's dental chart from 1938, and using video superimposition to match the skull with an old photograph of Mengele. The results indicated the corpse was almost certainly that of the missing and much-sought criminal, but in the absence of any positive proof, some doubt remained.

Only in 1992, when DNA samples from the corpse were compared with samples provided by Mengele's living relatives in Germany, was a positive correlation confirmed. The corpse was indeed Mengele's, and though he had managed to evade justice for the remainder of his life, the hunt was over at last.

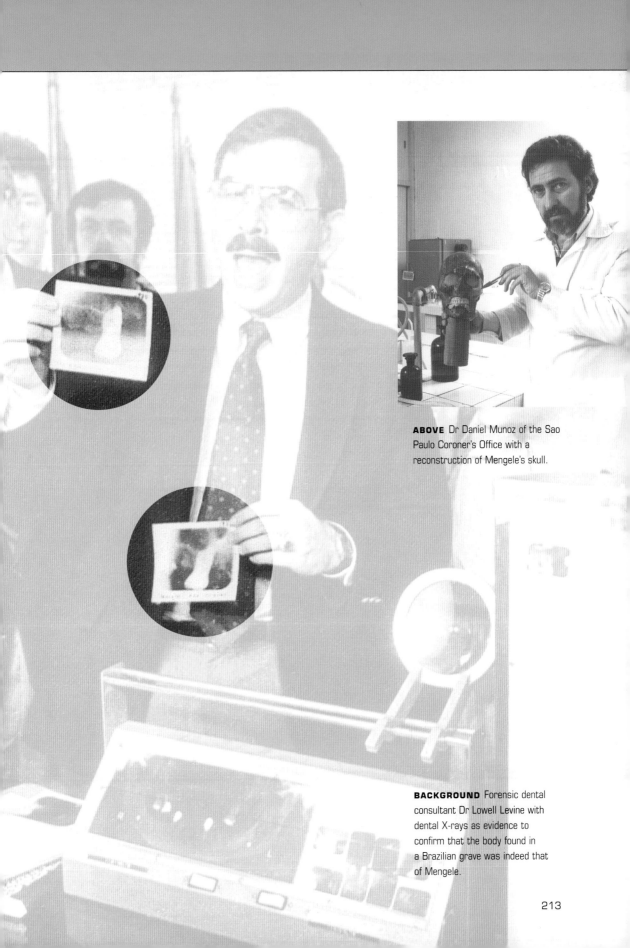

ABOVE Dr Daniel Munoz of the Sao Paulo Coroner's Office with a reconstruction of Mengele's skull.

BACKGROUND Forensic dental consultant Dr Lowell Levine with dental X-rays as evidence to confirm that the body found in a Brazilian grave was indeed that of Mengele.

The Tsar Nicholas II

BELOW Digging up the supposed remains of the Tsar and his family from marshy ground outside Ekaterinburg in 1993.

BELOW Tsar Nicholas II and the Tsarina Alexandra, with their children.

I n the violent civil war that followed Russia's October Revolution in 1917, the position of the Tsar and his immediate family became very precarious indeed. To the Communists, the family represented valuable bargaining chips—but they could also be seen as a potentially dangerous focus rallying for the Communists' White Russian enemies. By July 1918 the Imperial family was being held prisoner in the Ipatiev House in Ekaterinburg in Western Siberia. Their captors heard that White Russian forces were closing in and orders were received to execute the Tsar, his wife, his children, and the other members of their party. The bodies were to be disposed of where they would never be found.

During the late 1970s, when the official Soviet blackout on any discussion on the fate of Nicholas II and his family was still firmly in place, the house where they had been executed was demolished in an effort to stem the increasing flood of sightseers. But some factions were still searching for the remains of the murdered family. An Interior Ministry official, Gely Ryabov, managed to track down the son of one of the guards, Yakov Yurovsky, who had witnessed the shootings in the cellar of the Ipatiev house. Yurovsky's son told Ryabov that his father had described the burial as having taken place in marshy ground on the outskirts of the town.

Ryabov eventually located a mass grave which was covered by a layer of logs with earth piled on top. Working at night with a team of helpers, Ryabov dug below the logs and retrieved a pile of old and fragile bones, together with scraps of clothing, all of which he placed in hiding.

Not until 1991 was the political climate sufficiently relaxed for the team to make their discoveries public. In an effort to establish the identity of the remains, photographs of Tsar Nicholas and Tsarina Alexandra were superimposed on photographs of the two largest skulls: the results showed a promising likeness. But by then there was the possibility that DNA evidence could provide final confirmation.

In order to identify any DNA samples taken from the remains as belonging to the Tsar's family, DNA samples from someone known to be a direct descendant of a family member were needed. Because the bones had decayed, only a small amount of DNA was available, so examiners had to rely on a special type of DNA called mitochondrial DNA, which is passed on through the female parent in each generation. This narrowed the field of potential donors, but DNA samples were finally provided by Prince Philip, Duke of Edinburgh and husband of Queen Elizabeth II, who was descended from the Tsarina's sister.

Among the skeletons were those of a man, a woman, and their three children. When the DNA samples were compared with those of Prince Philip it became clear that the woman was

ABOVE Forensic scientist examining the bones thought to be those of the Tsar and the Imperial family.

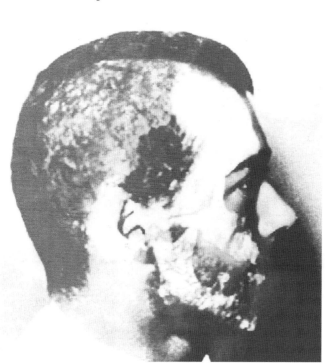

ABOVE Superimposing a photograph of the Tsarina on the second largest skull produced a close correlation.

LEFT Computer-generated image of a photo of Nicholas II superimposed on the largest skull found at the burial site, showing an equally close match.

RIGHT Chief researcher Dr. Peter Gill who verified the identity of the remains of the Imperial Family, was also asked to examine DNA from Anna Anderson Manahan, who claimed to be the Grand Duchess Anastasia whose remains had not been found (inset).

BELOW A medical expert locking the cases containing the remains of the Tsar and Tsarina and their children.

related to him, and therefore to the Tsarina's sister. This positively identified the bones as those of the Imperial family, though the skeletons of the young heir to the throne, the Tsarevich Alexei, and the Grand Duchess Anastasia were never found.

In a footnote to the main story, the fact that the bones of the Grand Duchess Anastasia were missing from the grave added new impetus to the story that the little girl had not been murdered with the rest of her family, but had escaped. It also focused attention on Anna Anderson, a refugee who had appeared in 1920 claiming to be Anastasia. Anderson's detailed knowledge of court life and of the Imperial family itself had convinced some of those who had known the family that her story was genuine.

Anna Anderson died in 1964, but by a remarkable coincidence some of her body tissue remained preserved in a hospital where she had undergone an operation shortly before her death. In 1994, DNA from her stored tissue was compared with that of the Tsar's children, and it was finally proved beyond doubt that she was not related to the family, and had certainly not been the Grand Duchess Anastasia. The mystery of Anastasia's eventual fate, like that of the Tsarevich Alexei, remains unresolved.

Anna Anderson's true identity was proved at last when members of the Schankowska family read of the DNA tests and claimed that the woman was a relative of theirs. She had been a penniless neurotic named Franzisca Schankowska who had reinvented herself as a member of the Imperial family and had earned a living from those she managed to dupe. Tests of DNA samples provided by the family showed that Anna Anderson had indeed been a close relative of theirs, and her true identity was exposed at last.

ABOVE Prince Philip, Duke of Edinburgh, a direct descendant of the Tsarina's sister, who provided DNA samples to help identify the remains.

BELOW Honor guard beside the coffins of the Tsar and his family, lying in state at the Petrovpavlovskaya Fortress in St. Petersburg before their ceremonial reburial.

The Future
of Forensic Science

ABOVE A magnifying glass over two DNA sequences.
The sequences, also known as an autoradiagram, is
four rows of irregularly spaced black bands.

Forensic science is now more powerful than it has ever been, and the evidence it produces promises to be increasingly reliable in the future, provided legitimate concerns about accuracy and civil liberties are properly addressed.

An individual can now be positively identified by a number of techniques other than DNA or fingerprint analysis. These include the use of bar and contour voiceprints, retinal scanning and the analysis of chemicals present in perspiration. In theory, all these different identifiers could be used to build up a database of criminal records that could be crossmatched to check evidence or help identify suspects.

The recording, sorting and management of such complex databases—as well as the systematic searching involved in locating matches—has been greatly facilitated by the introduction of computers. When data was stored on paper only, the task of matching fingerprints taken from a crime scene with those held in police files was long and laborious, and had to be undertaken by officers with specialist skills. In addition, if criminals

LEFT Forensic scientists examining fingerprint files in the National Fingerprint Gallery at the Metropolitan Police Support Headquarters in London, England, which contains more than 4.4 million fingerprint records.

BELOW A specialist fingerprint examiner working in 1948 with a magnifying glass to examine the type of print and determine the number of ridges. The result is recorded on the card and placed in the fingerprint files.

moved from their original area of operations, their prints did not necessarily appear on police records in their new neighborhood. Where the files from different police authorities were merged in a central system, the resulting databases were so unwieldy that a systematic search of the entire collection was beyond the resources of most police inquiries.

Indeed, as forensic science became more wide-ranging in the information it collects on those who commit a crime, sorting and processing that information became more and more time-consuming. Much of that development might well have been wasted, without the huge increase in the power and speed of computers.

The role of computers in crime fighting

The first force to use computers for storing fingerprint records was the Royal Canadian Mounted Police, which completed the process of computerizing its fingerprint files in 1973. Sweden followed in 1975, and a year later Germany's seventeen million criminal police records were transferred to a computer database. As more countries added their records, the possibilities of identifying and tracking down criminals on the basis of their prints became truly global.

Computer programs quickly became more efficient at searching out the fingerprints' points of classification and comparison, and capable of faster processing. By the 1990s,

fingerprint records could be scanned at rates of tens of thousands per second and the area and time frame of the search could easily be modified or enlarged.

Police were able for the first time to undertake "cold searches," looking for matches with prints found at the scene of a crime without having a particular suspect in mind. Because the system would quickly reveal any matches with the prints on file, investigators could let the computer do the searching. In addition, because fingerprint records were increasingly being shared between police forces, matches were being made that identified suspects in previously unsolved cases.

But this was just one aspect of the development of forensic computing. By the late 1980s both the British and American police were making use of powerful mainframe computers. Because these were highly efficient at searching out and identifying patterns, they could be fed with enormous amounts of data collected during the course of an investigation and used to reveal any statistical quirks that indicated a particular suspect or group of suspects that may be worth investigating.

ABOVE A forensic optical comparator for matching fingerprints.

RIGHT Using a hand-held scanner to feed paper fingerprint records into the computer database, where they can be compared side-by-side with suspect prints.

HOLMES and Floyd

In the United Kingdom, the first police national computer was developed during the 1970s to allow different forces all over the country to have access to a common bank of criminal records. In 1987 the British government introduced an additional computer system called the Home Office Large/Major Enquiry System (or HOLMES, after the great fictional detective). This allowed investigation teams to use the computer's pattern-sensing capabilities to suggest potential suspects, or to deliver a list of suspects who matched a series of characteristics revealed by forensic evidence at the scene of the crime.

In the United States, the FBI developed an "artificial-intelligence" computer system with the help of the Institute for Defense Analysis, part of the U.S. Department of Defense. This was called "Big Floyd," after the far-from-fictional Floyd Clark, head of the bureau's Criminal Identification Division, and it stored more than three million records belonging to the FBI Organized Crime Information System.

Big Floyd allows investigators to interrogate the computer to search for potential suspects or, if operators have a suspect in mind, the computer can reveal all the known information on that person. It can even suggest the next steps in investigating the subject, such as identifying known associates, approaching other sources of information or applying for permission for a wiretap for additional information in a particular area.

Some of the most difficult criminals to identify and track down are serial killers, who often find and strike their victims apparently at random. Two separate programs are being developed to help investigators generate psychological profiles of serial killers from the available evidence. One is run by the FBI's Behavioral Sciences Unit, which between 1979 and 1983 interviewed more than twenty convicted serial killers and their families. Detailed profiles were compiled and these are used to help identify other individuals showing similar patterns of behavior. The other program is the Violent Criminal Apprehension Program (VICAP) which was initiated by the FBI Academy in 1985. This records details of violent crimes, categorizing distinguishing features of each attack. Supplied with details of a new case, the program searches its records, comparing up to one hundred different features of each crime, to find the ten closest matches from its database. The resulting list is then analyzed by experts to assess whether the most recent crime may be one of a series committed by the same person.

TOP A technician using a barcode reader to enter fingerprint details into a computer file.

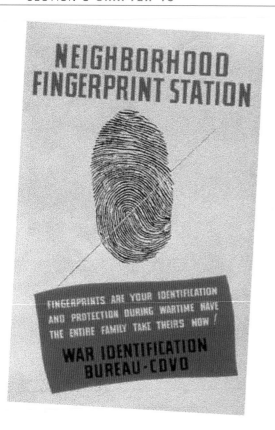

LEFT World War II poster highlighting a mass fingerprinting campaign for ordinary citizens.

ABOVE AND RIGHT An infrared viewer is used to examine a check. The numeral "1" has been altered to a "4."

Security screening

The one limitation common to all these computer records is that they can help to catch only those criminals who have had previous dealings with the police, so have had their details recorded. In several earlier cases (see pages 168 and 228), criminals were tracked down through mass fingerprinting and DNA testing that brought local people with no existing criminal records into the net. Suggestions that mass records such as these be retained and added to permanent police files invariably cause concerns regarding civil liberties. In today's increasingly security-conscious society, however, recorded evidence of individual identity is increasingly used to allow the ordinary citizen convenient access to sensitive parts of the workplace, to bank cash machines or other high-security areas.

For example, fingertip patterns can be scanned by computers to control access to secure areas of a plant or research establishment. A visitor simply presses a keypad, his or her print is automatically compared with the recorded prints of all authorized personnel, and if a match is found access is granted. Trials are already under way of futuristic cash-dispensing machines that use laser scans of customers' retinas in the same way to screen any user attempting to withdraw cash.

Equipment has also been developed that can detect forged signatures much more precisely than examination with the naked eye. The genuine signatory is required to sign on an electronic keypad that senses the pattern of the pressure and pen movements used. Although the pressure and pen movements may vary between consecutive signatures, the overall pattern remains the same. Though a skilled forger may be able to produce a convincing imitation of the genuine signature, he or she inevitably uses a different pattern of pressure and movement in doing so, and the equipment is able to detect this.

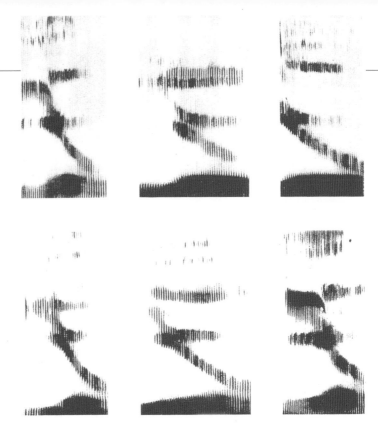

RIGHT Bar voiceprints showing a suspect saying the word "you" at top left. Five individuals repeated the word, and the positive match is shown at bottom right.

Bar and contour voiceprints

The characteristics of a person's voice, despite the prevalence of convincing mimics, are also highly individual. Voiceprints are made by recording two and a half seconds of a subject's speech on magnetic tape, then scanning the tape electronically to determine the different frequencies generated in the voice. The results are either displayed on a computer screen or drawn on a rotating drum by a moving stylus.

Two types of voiceprint display are used for security and identification purposes. Both show the time elapsed during the recording on the horizontal axis, and the different frequencies present in the voice on the vertical axis. The display most commonly used in giving evidence is the bar voiceprint, in which the intensity of the sound at different frequencies is shown by the density of the print at these different levels. The same information is presented in a different way in the contour voiceprint. Here the trace is presented as a pattern of lines joining together points of equal intensity, rather as contour lines on a map join together points of equal height to indicate three dimensions on a two-dimensional display.

In both cases, the patterns created by people with similar voices speaking the same words are still clearly distinguishable from one another. Moreover, when an individual attempts to disguise the voice by speaking at an unusually high or low pitch, the pattern may move vertically up or down the display, but it still shows the characteristic pattern and reveals the identity of the speaker when compared with the normal voice recording.

Voiceprints have been used in several cases in the U.S. to confirm the identity of telephone callers. They can also help identify, for example, a suspect who has made a ransom demand, left a threatening message or made a hoax call. The reliability of voiceprint identification was shown by tests carried out by the U.S. Air Force Systems Command in the early 1990s. A voice-recognition computer system was used to control access to secure areas. The system was found to be ninety-nine percent reliable, even when challenged by professional impersonators.

Individual identifiers

The need to identify individuals is not confined to criminal cases: a movement in the United States, sponsored by the American Dental Association in 1986, tried to persuade ordinary citizens to be "tagged" as part of a national register. Volunteers were invited to have a tiny disc bonded to a molar in the upper jaw. This almost indestructible identity marker would carry a unique twelve-digit code that could be read through a magnifier ... but so far only a minority of patients has taken up the offer.

In many cases, police have only witness descriptions on which to base their search for a suspect. Even now, some police forces use the services of skilled portrait artists who develop sketched likenesses of suspects from dialogue with the witness. However a more standardized system was developed as a result of suggestions by Hugh C. McDonald, chief of the civilian division of the Los Angeles Police Department, in 1940.

McDonald judged the traditional procedure to be both frustrating and time-consuming, and to speed things up he sketched a series of different kinds of eyes, noses, mouths, hairlines, face shapes and other individual features on transparent sheets so that they could be selected by the witness to assemble a picture of the suspect. This was the basis of

ABOVE LEFT A portrait artist developing the likeness of a suspect in discussion with a witness.

ABOVE RIGHT An Identikit researcher working with a crime victim to compose an image of the criminal's face.

the first Identikit system, which was commercially produced by the Townsend Company of Santa Ana in California. The original kit contained thirty-two different noses, thirty-three lips, one hundred and two pairs of eyes, fifty-two chins and twenty-five beards and mustaches. Using these elements together with different facial shapes it was possible to assemble sixty-two billion different faces. In addition, since each different feature was coded, information could be sent to other forces so that they could use the code to assemble their own equivalent Identikit portrait without seeing the original.

By the early 1960s, Identikit was being used by an increasing number of the world's police forces, but a successor was already being developed by forensic expert Jacques Penry from an idea he had conceived thirty years previously. In 1968, Penry was contracted by the Police Research and Development Branch of the British Home Office to produce a photographically-based facial identification system. Within a year, Penry produced a kit that had the potential to assemble five billion different male Caucasian faces. A year later he produced a supplement that could generate half a million Afro-Asian faces. Two years later, with the help of the Royal Canadian Mounted Police, he developed a kit that produced Native American faces, but the first Photofit kit for producing and identifying female faces took another two years to produce.

Since then, computers have played increasingly sophisticated roles in producing and identifying images. Specially designed software enables Photofit images to be produced in color and in three dimensions to give a more lifelike representation, and faces can be reconstructed from the blurred images retrieved from CCTV (close circuit television) security tapes by using image-enhancement facilities. Computer imagery has also been used—with some extraordinary success—in cases where the only physical likeness available is out of date and the image needs to be "aged" to resemble the subject's current appearance.

One program was developed by Scott Barrows and Lewis Sadler, two medical illustrators at the University of Illinois in Chicago. They used their anatomical

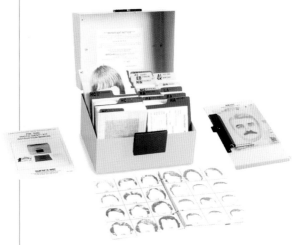

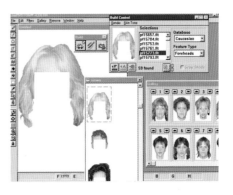

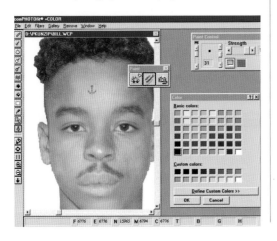

knowledge of how fourteen bones and more than one hundred muscles in the face develop as a person matures to project the probable appearance of a subject some years after the last known photograph was taken. The program is designed to suggest the physical changes that would naturally occur over time.

Researchers at the Louisiana State University have taken this technique a stage further in their Forensic Anthropology

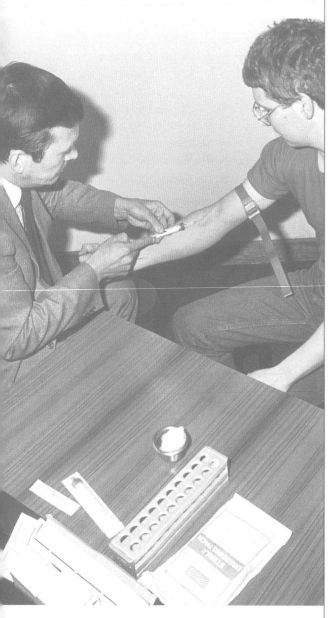

ABOVE A volunteer having a blood sample taken for police records.

Computer Enhanced System (FACES). This works by combining pictures of the subject with pictures of the parents, based on the concept that people from the same family tend to age in similar ways. The system has produced some remarkable identifications, especially in cases of child abductions where the child had been missing for some years.

Future possibilities— and pitfalls

Chromatography techniques are now so sensitive that they can produce a chemical spectrum of an individual's perspiration that is as unique as a fingerprint, and the possibility exists that the minuscule traces present in an individual's body odor may one day be enough to trigger a positive identification.

At present however, such information is useful only in proving that a known suspect was actually present at the scene where trace evidence was obtained. For these powerful techniques to assist detectives in finding their suspect in the first place, criminal records need to be redesigned and expanded to include all relevant information. Ideally, computers working from the evidence collected at the scene would be able to produce a short list of likely suspects in any given crime.

ABOVE A technician monitoring an analysis by high-performance liquid chromatography (HPLC).

There are already suggestions that criminals convicted of telephone offences—those involving threats, ransom demands or even just nuisance calls—should be required to have their voiceprints recorded at the same time as their fingerprints. In some states in the U.S., criminals give blood or saliva samples for DNA profiling as a standard part of their post-trial processing. However, extending this kind of record keeping to the wider public remains for the moment unlikely, given concerns over civil liberties and the potentially disastrous consequences of any errors made in the taking of samples or maintenance of records.

The increased sensitivity of the methods used in most fields of modern forensic science is not without its price. Those responsible for producing and assessing the evidence must be aware that their isolation of, or failure to identify, the merest trace of a particular chemical in a particular place can have direct

and devastating consequences. The highest scientific standards must be brought to bear at all times to guard against the possibility of accidental contamination of laboratory equipment, materials, or samples.

Some samples must be kept under strictly controlled conditions, for example, since any fluctuations in temperature can result in misleading test results. Future advances in this most demanding of scientific specializations are likely to concern the improved reliability, as well as the extended capability, of the techniques involved.

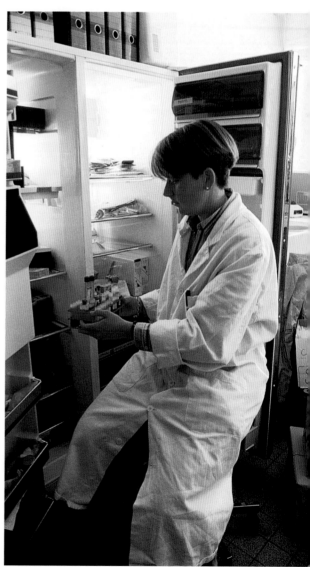

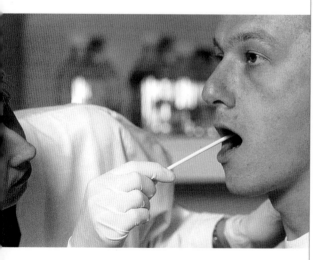

ABOVE Taking a saliva sample for DNA analysis.

RIGHT To prevent degradation and contamination of forensic samples, they are kept in secure refrigerators.

Richard Ramirez

Beginning in June 1984, a series of twelve violent murders were committed in Los Angeles. Each involved people being attacked in their homes in the middle of the night: male victims were shot, female victims raped. Several of the women were able to describe their attacker, named "The Nightstalker" by newspapers, as a tall, lean Hispanic man with bad teeth and body odor, but this information was not enough to provide promising leads when cross-matched with records of known sexual offenders.

There was a breakthrough in August 1985 when a victim managed to note down the number of the attacker's car as he drove away. A police hunt located the vehicle in a parking lot two days later; it had been stolen from outside a restaurant on the night of the previous attack. The car was put under surveillance, but the criminal did not return. Eventually it was searched by forensic examiners who found a single suspect fingerprint.

Because the Los Angeles Police Department's fingerprint records had been partly computerized earlier in the year, police were able to conduct a computer search, which retrieved a positive match. The subject was a Richard Ramirez, who had been fingerprinted following a minor traffic violation some years before. His photograph was circulated to the media, though Ramirez himself, who was out of town on a visit to Arizona to buy cocaine, was unaware of it.

On his return, he called at a liquor store on the East side of the city, to buy a can of cola and some doughnuts. Bystanders recognized him as the man whose face was printed on the newspapers in the racks at the store, and they chased him down the streets. Ramirez himself tried to evade his pursuers by stealing a car, but those chasing him were too close for his

BACKGROUND Richard Ramirez shows a pentagram on his left palm, a symbol of satanic worship, which had also been found at the scene of two of his crimes.

efforts to be successful. Finally he ran headlong into a waiting patrolman, also called Ramirez, and he was arrested.

Though Ramirez himself denied taking part in the crimes, during the three years it took for his trial to come to court he did all he could to change his appearance from the descriptions given by witnesses. It made little difference, as police searching the home of one of his friends had found the gun used in the murders, and jewelry belonging to his victims was found in the possession of Ramirez's sister.

On November 7, 1989, Ramirez was sentenced to death. He might never have been identified but for the computerized fingerprints records and his own date of birth. The records only covered criminals born since the 1st January 1960, and Ramirez had been born in February of that year.

ABOVE Elyas Abowath was one of "The Nightstalker's" victims.

BELOW Ramirez after his arrest on August 31, 1985—police believe he committed 24 brutal assaults and 16 murders.

Clifford Irving

By the 1970s the billionaire industrialist Howard Hughes had become a total recluse, living on a private island in the Bahamas. When in 1971 a writer named Clifford Irving claimed Hughes had agreed to his writing an authorized biography, publishers were skeptical. Only when letters signed by Hughes were pronounced genuine by Osborn, Osborn and Osborn, a company specializing in authenticating documents, did McGraw-Hill commission Irving to write the book and pay an enormous $765,000 advance to Hughes via a Swiss bank account.

The serialization rights to Irving's finished manuscript were sold to *Life* magazine. The magazine was then called by the Hughes Tool Company to arrange a telephone interview between Hughes and a group of radio, newspaper and television reporters. A conference call was set up in a Los Angeles hotel so that Hughes could answer detailed questions. For twenty minutes he was bombarded with queries, and his answers were recorded. Hughes insisted he had never met Irving, never given him permission to write his biography, and never received any payment.

Irving claimed the caller was an impostor, but since he had demonstrated detailed personal knowledge of Hughes in his answers to the reporters' questions, not everyone was convinced. The available evidence was re-examined. Letters purportedly from Hughes and amendments he had allegedly made to drafts of the book were shown to R.A. Cabbane, a document examiner for

BELOW Howard Hughes, pictured before his retreat into seclusion.

BELOW RIGHT Forged signatures of Howard Hughes shown on the top two lines showed several points of resemblance to Irving's own handwriting, shown in the remaining lines.

the U.S. Postal Service, along with samples of Irving's own handwriting. Though the signatures on the letters were very similar to the genuine article, they were now exposed as high-quality fakes. Experts also detected a resemblance between the formation of some of the letters in the forged signatures and that in Irving's own writing.

Investigators then set about establishing whether or not the conference caller had been genuine. Voiceprints made from the recorded interview were compared with voiceprints made from a recording of a speech Hughes had made in 1947 to a Senate sub-committee. The prints were compared by Lawrence G. Kersta, who had produced the first voiceprints while working at the Bell Telephone Laboratories in New Jersey in 1963. He found the two prints were almost certainly produced by the same person, and his findings were confirmed by Dr. Peter Ladefoged, Professor of Phonetics at U.C.L.A., whose assessment took into account the difference in the subject's age at the times the two recordings were made.

BELOW Clifford Irving and his wife Edith.

Finally, a report was received from Swiss bank officials who were alarmed that their establishment had unwittingly played a role in the fraud. An account had been opened at the bank in the name of Helga R. Hughes shortly before a check had been deposited by McGraw-Hill, made payable to H. R. Hughes. The account had been opened by Irving's wife.

The couple were tried for fraud and on June 16, 1972, and Irving was sentenced to two and a half years in prison. His wife, found guilty of being an accessory, was sentenced to serve eighteen months.

O.J. Simpson

O n June 12, 1994, Nicole Simpson-Brown, former wife of football star O.J. Simpson, and her friend Ronald Goldman were found dead just inside the front gate of Mrs. Simpson's home. Both bodies were covered in blood and showed deep knife wounds. Simpson himself was ordered to report to the police, but he fled in a friend's car before eventually returning to give himself up.

When Simpson was eventually charged with both murders, it appeared that the forensic evidence against him was overwhelming and the outcome of the trial a foregone conclusion. Drops of blood were found at the scene that did not match the blood groups of either of the victims but had at least three factors in common with Simpson's blood—a trait shared by

RIGHT O.J. Simpson with his ex-wife Nichole Simpson-Brown and their children Sidney and Justin.

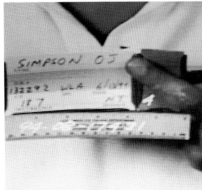

ABOVE The cut on Simpson's left hand that police noticed the day after the killings.

only one in two hundred of the population. When DNA profiling was carried out on blood drops found on the rear gate of Mrs. Simpson's property, the match with O.J. Simpson's blood was so close that only one person in fifty-seven billion could be expected to produce an equivalent match.

These incriminating drops were found near a set of bloody size twelve footprints that reproduced the sole pattern of a rare design of Bruno Magli shoes. Not only were these prints from shoes of Simpson's size, but photographs were produced at the later civil trial showing him wearing shoes of that particular design. When interviewed by police on the day after the killings, Simpson was also seen to have a cut on his left hand. A bloodstained left-hand glove was discovered next to the bodies and it bore traces of fibers from Goldman's jeans and shirt; the matching right-hand glove, with traces of Simpson's blood, was found outside his own home. Traces of the victims' blood were also found inside Simpson's car and home.

Unfortunately for the prosecution, the forensic evidence was largely wasted. Simpson's defense attorneys argued that the attitudes of the police officers involved implied a racist bias against their client, and hinted at police corruption. They also cast doubts on the methods used by the forensic laboratories involved and the professionalism of those responsible for collecting, preserving and testing the forensic evidence. Much was made of the absence of a murder weapon and the dearth of eyewitness testimony. Independent witnesses were also found

ABOVE Expert officer Gregory Matheson of the LAPD gave jurors a detailed explanation of the DNA testing methods, earlier believed flawless and foolproof in determining the guilt or innocence of O.J. Simpson.

BELOW Gregory Matheson shows a diagram of six EAP phenotypes to the jury, as part of his explanation of DNA methods.

Block Diagram Showing the Six EAP Phenotypes

who testified to having seen Simpson on the day of the murders. The timing of their sightings indicated that he could not have been at the scene long enough to have carried out the killings.

Dr. Henry Lee, director of the Connecticut Forensic Science Laboratory, also appeared to admit under cross-examination that ambiguous blood traces found at the scene could have been partial shoe-prints made by a different sole pattern. If true, this suggested another killer may have been present, which clearly damaged the case against Simpson. Though FBI experts testified that the marks Dr. Lee referred to were not shoe prints at all, the prosecution case had lost credibility, and Simpson was eventually acquitted.

Nevertheless, a civil prosecution was later brought by the victims' families and the case was effectively retried: this time Simpson was found responsible for both deaths and ordered to pay huge sums in damages. This second trial appeared to confirm the value of the evidence, but the original case remains a powerful reminder that forensic science can be successfully brought to bear only when the evidence is collected, analyzed and presented according to the highest professional standards.

BACKGROUND Crime scene photograph of the body of Nicole Simpson-Brown.

BELOW Defendant O.J. Simpson wearing the gloves found by Los Angeles police. The prosecutors sought to prove that the gloves fitted Simpson's hands.

The New Bedford Highway Murders

On July 3, 1988, outside Freetown near New Bedford, Massachusetts, the partially mummified body of a young woman was found close to Highway 140.

This victim seems to have been the first in a series of killings now known as the New Bedford Highway Murders. On July 30, 1988, the skeleton of another young woman was found near Interstate 195.

The first body was eventually identified from dental records as that of Debra Medeiros. In the meantime a third body had been found and, concerned that there may be more undiscovered bodies in the area, police from both Massachusetts and Connecticut mounted a search using tracker dogs. A fourth body was found on November 29, a fifth just two days later, and a sixth was discovered on December 10.

Dental records identified the second body, and a partial fingerprint identified the fourth victim. Several of the victims had backgrounds of prostitution and drug addiction, as well as links with the New Bedford Portuguese community.

Another body was found on March 28, 1989, body number eight was found on March 31, and number nine was unearthed on April 24.

New Bedford prostitutes were interviewed and a number of women claimed to have been attacked by a man working in law enforcement. The man had tried to strangle them. One woman claimed that a man driving a white pick-up truck had raped her near a highway exit close to where three of the bodies had been found. A thirty-five-year-old man had been identified, arrested, and charged with the rape, and police began to suspect that he might also be responsible for the killings.

In spite of these leads, the forensic evidence from a total of nine bodies has so far not provided a positive link to any one of the suspects, and to date no one has been arrested and charged with the New Bedford Highway Murders. The file remains open after more than ten years. And this of course is not the only case still waiting for a conclusion: the so-called Green River killer in King County, Washington, is thought to be responsible for the murder of more than forty prostitutes, but so far no one has been found and charged. For all the power of modern forensic science, some serial killers still manage to elude identification and capture—just as Jack the Ripper did more than a century ago.

ABOVE Fingerprint records.

Acid phosphatase test: Test that uses two substances to reveal the presence of seminal fluid by the appearance of a purple color.

AFIS: Automated Fingerprint Identification Systems, which enable computers to make rapid and accurate comparisons between fingerprints and the vast numbers of fingerprints in police records.

Agglutination: The tendency of red blood cells to mass together in clumps in reaction to the presence of an antibody.

Antigens: Chemicals that are attached to the surface of the red blood cells to create the different blood groups.

Arches: One of the characteristic patterns of ridges in a fingerprint, possessed by around 5 percent of the population.

Ballistics: The examination of firearms and the projectiles they discharge, in relation to crime.

Benzidine color test: A test formerly used to reveal the presence of blood at the scene of a crime.

Bertillonage: A method of classifying human beings by a set of detailed body measurements, invented by Alphonse Bertillon, a clerk in the French Sûreté in 1883, but rendered obsolete by fingerprinting.

Big Floyd: The FBI supercomputer that contains software allowing it to search criminal records and draw conclusions from the available information in the hunt for those responsible for an individual crime.

Blasting cap: A small explosive charge triggered by lighting a safety fuse or applying an electric current, used to detonate high explosives.

Blood group: A classification system that divides human blood into groups A, B, AB and O, according to the antibodies and antigens carried by the red blood cells.

Bullet wipe: A dark ring-shaped mark made up of lead, carbon oil and dirt brushed from a bullet as it enters the skin, and found around the entry wound.

Caliber: The internal diameter of the barrel of a firearm, and the bullets it fires.

Choke: The constriction of the barrel of a shotgun to reduce the spread of shot as it leaves the gun, to increase its effective range.

Chromosomes: 23 pairs of threadlike bodies found in the nucleus of most human cells that carry the genes.

Comparison microscope: Two compound microscopes (see below) formed into a single unit, so that objects placed under each objective can be compared side by side in a single eyepiece.

Compound microscope: The basic microscope that uses two lenses (or combinations of lenses), an objective lens and an eyepiece lens, to focus a greatly magnified image of the subject on the retina of the observer's eye.

Concentric fractures: Patterns of cracks in glass pierced by a missile like a bullet, which run between the radial fractures (see below) and which originate on the side of the glass from which the impact came.

Cortex: The middle layer of human hair containing the particles of pigment that give the hair its individual color.

Cuticle: The protective outer sheath of the hair, formed by a series of overlapping scales.

Delta: A characteristic junction in the looped ridge patterns seen in the fingerprints of approximately 65 percent of people.

Density Gradient Tube: Equipment for measuring the distribution of particles of different density in a soil sample by determining the point at which they are suspended in a glass tube filled with successive layers of liquid of different densities.

Dental records: A standard system for classifying person's teeth according to distribution, displacement, and their appearance, together with any gaps or evidence of remedial work, useful for identifying bodies because of the virtual indestructibility of the teeth.

Depressants: Drugs that depress the action of the central nervous system such as phenobarbital, pentobarbital and alcohol.

Diatoms: Microscopic organisms found in lake and river water, which reveal by their presence whether a victim found in these surroundings died by drowning, or was already dead on entering the water.

DNA: Deoxyribonucleic acid, the molecules of which carry the body's genetic blueprint, and which provide a unique identifier for each individual.

Double action: A gun action where the pulling of the trigger to fire a round re-cocks the gun so that the next round is ready to be fired. (compare this with Single action, see below).

Dry drowning: Death caused by a body reflex from a spasm of the larynx due to the shock of the victim falling into the water, resulting in the heart stopping.

Electron microscope: A microscope that forms its image by the electrons emitted from the specimen when scanned by a focused beam of electrons.

Femur: The thighbone, which can be measured and used as a guide to the height of the person to whom it belonged.

Fingertip search: The careful, inch by inch combing of the crime scene by a team of searchers to turn up the smallest items of forensic evidence.

Forensic anthropologist: Specialist who can determine whether or not bones or other remains are human in origin and, if so, reveal details about how the victim died and how they appeared in life.

Forensic chemist: Specialist in the analyses of drugs, dyes, paint samples and other chemicals involved in crimes.

Forensic dentist: Specialist in examining the teeth of murder or accident victims for identification purposes, and for comparison with bite-mark evidence at crime scenes.

Forensic document investigator: Specialist in examining forged documents and forged signatures.

Forensic entomologist: Specialist in the different types of insect life which may be found on corpses or at murder scenes, as an indication of the time, season and weather when a crime may have been committed.

Forensic geologist: Specialist in the characteristics of soil samples, and what these can reveal in terms of the movements of a victim or a suspect.

Forensic pathologist: Specialist pathologist responsible for carrying out autopsies of murder victims and recording of evidence found on or in the body as to the manner and time of death.

Forensic photographer: Specialist who records forensic evidence on film at the crime scene or in the forensic laboratory.

Forensic psychiatrist/psychologist: Experts who evaluate a murder scene and victim to produce a possible psychological profile of the murderer.

Forensic serologist: Specialist in the study of blood and other bodily fluids in addition to DNA for identifying possible suspects.

Gas chromatography: A technique for separating complex mixtures of substances according to their movement when carried by gas through a thin film of liquid.

Gel electrophoresis: A method of testing for human blood by the movement of antibodies and antigens on a gel-coated plate subjected to an electrical field.

Hallucinogens: Drugs like marijuana, LSD, PSP and Ecstasy, which produce changes in mood, thought and perception.

High explosives: Explosives that produce an extremely intense explosive effect and a supersonic pressure wave when they detonate.

HOLMES: Acronym for the Home Office Large/Major Enquiry System, the UK mainframe police computer system.

Identikit: The first packaged system for reconstructing the appearance of suspects' faces, based on a wide choice of drawings of facial features.

Iodine fumes: The oldest method for visualizing latent fingerprints at a crime scene.

Latent fingerprints: Fingerprints at a crime scene that are present but not visible until visualized through one of several different techniques, including iodine fuming.

Liquid chromatography: Technique for separating complex mixtures into their constituents by dissolving the mixture in solution and passing it through a finely divided absorbent material.

Livor mortis: A coloration of the skin of the lower parts of a corpse, caused by the settling of the red blood cells as the blood ceases to circulate.

Low explosives: Explosives having a detonation less violent than high explosives (above) and that produce a subsonic pressure wave.

Luminol: A substance that can be sprayed onto furnishings at a crime scene to reveal traces of blood as spots of bright light.

Mass spectrometry: A technique for identifying the constituent parts of a mixture by passing their molecules through a high-vacuum chamber where they acquire a positive charge through colliding with a beam of electrons, which separates them according to their different masses.

Mitochondrial DNA: A type of DNA found in particular structures of the body and passed on intact through the female line of descent.

Narcotics: Drugs that have a painkilling or analgesic effect and can create a physical dependence among regular users.

Neutron activation analysis: Technique for identifying substances by bombarding a sample with neutrons in a nuclear reactor,

and measuring the energies and intensities of the resulting gamma rays.

Nucleotides: The basic building blocks of the DNA helix, each consisting of one of four types of base (adenine, cytosine, guanine or thymine) attached to a sugar-phosphate group.

Phenolphthalein: A substance used with hydrogen peroxide to test for the presence of blood at a crime scene, which is revealed as a deep pink color.

Phrenology: A later discredited theory first proposed in 1796 that the shape of the head revealed different facets of the individual's personality through the presence of bumps and irregularities.

Plasma: The basic fluid constituent of blood, which carries the different blood cells.

Polymer: A complex long-chain molecule containing many repeated units or monomers.

Polymerase Chain Reaction (PCR): A technique that replicates part of a DNA strand outside a living cell, eventually producing millions of copies from the smallest original sample.

Portrait parlé: A system for regularizing verbal descriptions of a suspect's facial features introduced in the 1890s to aid positive identification.

Preciptin test: A test to confirm that a blood sample is of human origin by treating it with human anti-serum.

Prostate Specific Antigen (PSA): A substance contained in human seminal fluid that allows a test to confirm the presence of human semen.

Protein: Polymers made up of amino acids that are the basic building blocks of living organisms.

Pump-action: A shotgun carrying several cartridges in an internal magazine, and which can be reloaded by simply pushing a slider backwards and forwards.

Radial: A loop formed as part of a fingerprint pattern which opens towards the thumb.

Radial fractures: Fractures that form a star shape when a sheet of glass is pierced by a bullet, and which originate on the side opposite to the initial impact.

Rhesus factor: An additional way of differentiating between the blood of different individuals, who may be Rhesus positive or Rhesus negative, according to the presence or absence of a particular antibody.

Rigor mortis: The stiffness of the body after death, which helps in reconstructing the time at which

death occurred.

Sciatic notch: Characteristic shape of part of the hipbone which can indicate whether a skeleton is that of a male or female.

Secretor: An individual who carries his or her blood group information in all their body fluids, including for example saliva and sweat.

Single-action: A type of revolver which needs to be cocked before each shot by pulling back the hammer (see Double action).

Stimulants: Drugs which increase the activity of the central nervous system, creating feelings of confidence and energy.

Striations: Fine lines in the internal rifling of a firearm caused by the cutting tool, which impart an individual identity to the gun, and to any bullets fired from it.

Superglue fuming: A technique for visualizing latent fingerprints on non-porous surfaces by using cyanoacrylate ester fumes.

Tattooing: A characteristic pattern in the skin caused by particles of unburned and partly burned powder from a shotgun blast at very close range.

TESTED: A mnemonic used by air accident investigators searching for the main parts of a crashed aircraft (Tips of the wings and tail surfaces, Engines, control Surfaces, Tail assembly, External devices like landing gear and Doors).

Thin-layer chromatography: Technique for separating a mixture into its constituent parts by the speed at which they move by capillary action up a plate coated with a thin layer of silica gel.

Tibia: The shin-bone, which can be used as a guide for calculating the height of a person.

Toxicology: The study of poisons, their effects and symptoms and tests to reveal their use.

Ulnar: A loop pattern on a fingerprint which has its open end towards the little finger (see radial).

Vitreous humor: The fluid that fills the eyeball and shows changes after death, which can be used as an accurate way of identifying the time of death.

Whorls: Fingerprint patterns where the ridges turn through at least one complete circuit.

X-rays: Electromagnetic radiation of high energy and very high frequency which can penetrate most materials to different extents and reveal their underlying structure.

Acknowledgments

It's always difficult to remember in the course of a book covering a subject as broad (and in many areas, as detailed) as *Hidden Evidence* all the many people who helped along the way with advice, encouragement and information. Starting with those who played a crucial role in bringing the book from an initial concept to a finished volume, in broadly chronological order, I should like to thank Roddie Craig for the original inspiration, Diana Steedman who turned the idea into a structured plan, Veneta Bullen who undertook the mammoth task of sourcing and identifying pictures, Diane Pengelly who subjected the text to detailed scrutiny and last, but most definitely not least, Toria Leitch for bringing the whole thing together in its finished form. To all of them, I send my sincere and grateful thanks, as I do to the anonymous but ever-helpful staff of the Reference Library of the City of Liverpool for tracking down the most detailed and elusive information for what has been a demanding but rewarding book to write.

David Owen - *January 2000.*

Bibliography

Air Accident Investigation: How Science is making Flying Safer, David Owen, *Newbury Park, California, Haynes Publishing, 1998.*
Beyond the Crime Lab: the New Science of Investigation, Jon Zonderman, *New York, John Wiley & Sons, 1999 (revised edition).*
The Blooding, Joseph Wambaugh, *New York, Bantam Books, 1989.*
The Casebook of Forensic Detection, Colin Evans, *New York, John Wiley & Sons, 1996.*
Criminalistics, Richard Saferstein, *New York, Prentice Hall (various editions).*
Detecting Forgery: the Forensic Investigation of Documents, Joe Nickell, *University of Kentucky Press, 1996.*
The Encyclopedia of Forensic Science, Brian Lane, *London, England, Hodder Headline, 1992.*
How to Solve a Murder: the Forensic Handbook, Michael Kurland, *New York, Macmillan, 1995.*
Lockerbie, David Johnston, *London England, Bloomsbury, 1989.*
Simpson's Forensic Medicine, Bernard Knight, *London, England, Arnold, 1996.*

Picture credits

The publisher would like to thank the following for permission to reproduce their images. While every effort has been made to ensure this listing is correct the publisher apologises for any omissions or errors.

Fotomas Index: p9(b), p10(b), p88, p97(b)
Black Museum: p 3(l and r), p10(t,tr), p16, p25, p29 and 5(l), p32, p49(t), p 58(t), p66(t), p83(b) and 7(t), p 97(t), p110(b), p116(r), p119(r), p126, p127(b), p133, 161(t), p166(b), p173(b), p175(t), p231
Science Photo Library: p11(t) Phillipe Plailly, p11(b) Peter Menzel, p20 Jean-Loup Charmet, p47, p62(t) Tony Craddock, p62(b) Gary Watson, p70(t) John Greim, p72, p73(t and b) Dr. Jurgen, p74 James King-Holmes, p85, p96, p103 Manfred Kage, p111(b) Professor Harold Edgerton, p114(c) and p115 Stephen Dalton, p119(l) and 7(c) Michel Viard, p146(b) Klaus Guldlbrandsen, p147(b) Robert Holgmren, p148(t) Volker Sleger, p151(r) and 1(r) Tony Craddock, p152(b) Geoff Tompkinson, p160 Alfred Pasieka, p163 Philipe Plailly, p177(t) and 1(l) Dr. Jurgen, p177(b) Andrew Syred, p178(c) Andrew Syred, p178(b) Dr. Jeremy Burgess, p179(bl) and p180(bl) Astrid & Hans Friedler, p180(br) Andrew Syred, p181(b) Manfred Kage, p187 Andrew Syred, p190(b) Dr. Jurgen, p191 P. Leca, p192(t), p192(b) Michel Viard, Peter Arnold, p193(t) Robert Longehaye, p193(b) CC Studio, p194(t) David Parker, p194(b) Peter Menzel, p196(cl) Carlos Goldin, p197 Dr. Jurgen, p200 Robert Longehaye, p201(b) A Barrington Brown, p202(t) and 3(c) Professor Ke Seddon & Dr. T Evans, p203 Alfred Pasieka, p204 and 1(c) Philippe Plailly, p205(l) and p207(b) Peter Menzel, p205(r) and p206(b) Michael Gilbert, p207(t) David Parker, p218, p219(t) Peter Menzel, p221, p224(r) and p227(r) Michael Viard & Peter Arnold, p226(r) Geoff Tompkinson
Science and Society Picture Library: p13(l and r), **Hulton Getty:** p14(b and c), p15(bl), p17, p21(tr), p22, p24(t), p65, p69(t), p76, p77(t), p147(t), p149, p152(t), p158(t) **Roger Viollet:** p15(r), p19, p21(bl and br), p23(l), p98-9 **Frank Spooner:** p2, p23(r), p44, p46, p48, p49(b), p51, p53, p60(t), p61(t), p63, p64(r), p67(cl and b), p68(b),

p69(b), p70(b), p71, p92(b), p106, p107(t), p108(t and b), p109(b), p113(tr), p114(t), p117, p120(t), p122(l and r), p123(c), p129(b), p135, p136(tl), p138, p139, p140, p141(t and c), p142, p143(c), p144, p145(t), p146(t), p153, p158(b), p167(b), p181(t), p188(b), p189(b), p204(b), p213(r), p214(t), p215(t), p216(t), p224 and 6(b), p227(l), p233, p235
Corbis: p24(b), p36, p37, p39(t), p42(tl), p43(r), p59(t), p60(b), p81(t), p86-7, p105(t), p112(t and bl), p120(b), p121(l), p123(b), p125(b), p128, p129(t), p171(tr), p172, p173(t), p198, p201(t), p212(t), p219(c) and 6(t), 220(b), p222(tl), p228-9, p230
Rex Features: p26, p27(t), p28, p33 and 7(b), p45, p53 and 6(l), p63, p64(r), p66(b), p68(t), p82 and 5(c), p84, p89, p95(b), p104, p111(t), p112(br), p113, p116(l), p118 and 5(r), p123(t), p127(t and c), p134, p136 (tr and b), p137, p141(b), p155, p174, p179(t), p189(t), p206(t)
Popperfoto: p27(bl), p38, p39(b), p40-41, p42, p43(l), p55(t), p56, p58(b), p59(b), p61(b), p77(c and b), p109(t), p143(cl), p145(b), p156, p157, p159, p170, p171(tl and b), p188(t), p212(b), p213(l), p214(b), p215(bl and br), p 216(b and tl), p217, p 232(r), p234
Sirchi Fingerprint Laboratory: p27(br), p31(b), p161(c and b), p162, p164-5, p166(t), p167(t), p190(t), p196(cr), p220(t), p222(tr), p225 **Oxford Scientific Films:** p30
International Civil Aviation Organisation, Quebec: p35
Jerry Young: p52 **Wilf Gregg:** p54, p55(m and b), p57, p75
The Art Archive: p67(t), p110(t), p121(r)
Topham: p78, p79, p124(t and b), p125(t), p169, p182-3, p184-6, p199, p210(t), p211 **Jonathan Goodman:** p90, 150
Solo Syndication: p81(b), p80
James Lawrence: p89(b), p102, p105(b), p176(t), p196(t), p202(b), p203(l) **Royal Society:** p 12
Robert Harding: p100, p107(bl and br), p130
Dr Nic Daeid: p131, p132, p175(r), p176(bl and br)
Foster & Freeman: p154(t) **British Textile:** p178(t)
Neville Chadwick: p208-9, p226(l) **Mercury Press:** p210(c)